The Idea of Suicide

This book is about a new theory of suicide as cultural mimesis, or as an idea that is internalized from culture. Written as part of a new, critical focus in suicidology, this volume moves away from the dominant, strictly scientific understanding of suicide as the result of a mental disorder, and towards positioning suicide as an anthropologically salient, community-driven phenomenon. Written by a leading researcher in the field, this volume presents a conception of suicide as culturally scripted, and it demonstrates how suicide becomes a cultural idiom of distress that for some can become a normative option.

Michael J. Kral is an associate professor in the School of Social Work at Wayne State University, USA.

Researching Social Psychology

The Idea of Suicide
Contagion, Imitation, and Cultural Diffusion

Michael J. Kral

Routledge
Taylor & Francis Group

NEW YORK AND LONDON

First published 2019
by Routledge
52 Vanderbilt Avenue, New York, NY 10017

and by Routledge
2 Park Square, Milton Park, Abingdon, Oxon, OX14 4RN

First issued in paperback 2020

Routledge is an imprint of the Taylor & Francis Group, an informa business

© 2019 Taylor & Francis

The right of Michael J. Kral to be identified as author of this work
has been asserted by him in accordance with sections 77 and 78 of
the Copyright, Designs and Patents Act 1988.

Library of Congress Cataloguing-in-Publication Data
A catalog record for this book has been requested

ISBN 13: 978-0-367-67065-8 (pbk)
ISBN 13: 978-0-367-02659-2 (hbk)

Typeset in Sabon
by Apex CoVantage, LLC

To Ed Shneidman,
mentor and friend,
and to your postself.

Contents

Preface

This book is a theory of suicide. It is a cultural theory, and there are no cultural theories of suicide. The closest may be Emile Durkheim's sociological theory, seeing suicide as a result of too low or too high social integration and regulation, or social belonging/inclusion and the rules of a society or life compass. As the reader will see, however, I do not think this is a theory of suicide, but merely a theory of perturbation. These are social reasons that can upset people, but not necessarily drive them to suicide. My theory sees being upset or perturbed as one of two necessary ingredients for suicide. Being upset does not lead to suicide, but to doing something about it. The other ingredient in my theory is lethality or the idea of suicide. One has to choose suicide as the method to end the perturbation. The idea of suicide comes from where most of our ideas come from: culture. There are cultural models of suicide that are internalized by vulnerable, perturbed people. We imitate each other in so many things, and we imitate each other in suicide. I look at the theory of Gabriel Tarde to show that imitation is how culture works, and suicide is part of culture.

Chapter 1 looks at how humans imitate each other. There is much evidence for this, from developmental and social psychology to neurobiology. We begin to imitate others from infancy. We internalize cultural models of just about everything, from how we eat, how close we stand to each other, to what we wear, how we display our emotions. Cultural traits can spread from one society to another and from one person to another, and this is called diffusion. It can be conscious or unconscious. This chapter also examines the new field of critical suicidology, which questions the narrow focus of suicidology on mental illness and the individual through quantitative research. Critical suicidology takes on contextual, social justice, feminist, qualitative, queer, historical, subjective, ecological, and political perspectives.

Chapter 2 examines social epidemics. People in large groups can copy each other, and again this is how culture works. Contagion and imitation are seen across most human endeavors. We will see episodes of what is called mass hysteria, often seen in schools, workplaces, and even in the history of witch-hunting. Chapter 3 identifies other approaches to suicide, including historical, biological, psychological, sociological, and anthropological. Durkheim and the sociological view of suicide is discussed in detail. Suicide has been viewed many different ways over time and has moved from being seen as free will to one being determined by factors such as mental illness or stress. Chapter 4 is on suicide and culture from an anthropological perspective. I link psychology and anthropology, or mind and culture, showing how suicide is a very cultural phenomenon. I outline my theory in this chapter in some detail, looking at how the idea of suicide is learned through culture, how it is imitated and is contagious. I also look at how suicide differs across cultures. Chapter 5 is about Gabriel Tarde's theory and how it applies to suicide. There is currently a revival of Tarde's theory as it is being incorporated into contemporary social theory.

Acknowledgments

This book has been years in the making. I thank Ludek Broz, Daniel Münster, and two anonymous reviewers for their comments and suggestions on earlier drafts of this book. I especially thank Seth Abrutyn and Ian Marsh for commenting on the entire manuscript. I also thank the late Edwin Shneidman, my mentor from UCLA, who very much supported me in developing my idea expressed here. This was even though he knew I disagreed with his belief that psychological pain or psychache, as he called it, causes suicide. I appreciate the sabbatical granted to me by Wayne State University so that I could work on this book.

1 Introduction

Human Imitation as Culture

People have tried to understand suicide for a very long time. It has been studied by psychology, psychiatry, sociology, public health, and recently anthropology. Freud called suicide a riddle. It is indeed a puzzle. One frame to see suicide has been psychological, which Shneidman (1993) saw as extreme and unbearable psychological pain, what he called psychache, looking into the mind, phenomenologically. This view has been very productive. Pompili (2018) shows that there are four theoretical models of suicide: the scientific, determinist view such as mental illness causing suicide; the "cry for help" view where the person wants to reduce their distress; the sociogenic view, such as that of Durkheim who believed that social forces and society lead to suicide; and a stress-diathesis model where environmental stress interacts with a vulnerable individual. As James Hillman (1964, p. 16) asks about suicide, "How can one understand it? Why does one do it? Why does one not?" He calls suicide one of the human possibilities, where death can be chosen. There are a number of theories of suicide, but I refer to most of these as theories of perturbation, of distress. We have a long list of suicide risk factors, but they only mean that the person is upset, not suicidal. Most people with these risk factors are not suicidal. In this book a new theory of suicide is proposed. It is a cultural theory, seeing suicide as an idea internalized from culture by vulnerable people. We will turn to a view of culture as imitation, diffusion, and contagion, which will then lead to seeing suicide this way. Cheng, Hong, Silenzio, and Caine (2014) see imitation as the best explanation for suicide contagion.

Why do humans do what they do? Is much of what we do innate, something we were born with? Or are we tabula rasa, a blank slate, where everything we do is learned? Psychology has a very long history of looking into these questions, and the answer is usually both. We are born with certain features, and we learn a great deal. In this book we will see how much we actually learn from our environment, from our culture. We will see that most of what we do is culturally learned, and we lea~ from each other. Benedict (1953) called this cultural conditioning. M ray and Kluckhohn (1953) argued that all human behavior is cultu determined, as did Boas (2013/1910, p. 8), who wrote that behavior is determined "by the habitual reactions of the society to which the individual in question belongs." We copy each other. How you hold and drink a cup of tea, how you speak to others, how you think about yourself, are all learned from our culture. We are culturally constructed beings. Let us begin with imitation as a way that culture works, as the way we learn most everything.

Imitation is something we all do, and have done all our lives. Imitation is how culture works. It makes us who we are. This book is about a new theory of suicide as cultural mimesis, as an idea that is internalized from culture and imitated (Kral, 1994, 1998). I wrote the first paper on this theory in 1994, when culture was not very much included in suicidology. That year I began a cultural study of suicide among Inuit in Arctic Canada, so culture was on my mind. I read the 1904 book *Social Logic* by Gabriele Tarde and began to think about suicide from the perspective of imitation. Once I thought of suicide in this way, I could not return to my old way of thinking of suicide as caused by risk factors and mental illness. I had never thought that before and had been working on suicide and suicide prevention for years. After that, I could no longer see suicide any other way. Suicide had a new image.

The understanding of suicide, or suicidology, is dominated by psychology and psychiatry, and is seen as individualized, narrowly focused on risk factors, caused by a mental disorder, and the study of it is strictly scientific, marked by positivist quantitative research (Marsh, 2010). Most of the research on suicide is focused on these factors and methods, and most theories of suicide also look at this. Suicidology is in the tradition of positivist/empiricist science. The individual focus is paramount. As Gould (1981, pp. 22–23) wrote,

> Scientists can struggle to identify the cultural assumptions of their trade and to ask how answers might be formulated under different assertions. But science's potential as an instrument for identifying the cultural constraints upon it cannot be fully realized until scientists give up the twin myths of objectivity and inexorable march toward truth. . . . The most creative theories are often imaginative visions imposed upon facts; the source of imagination is also strongly cultural.

What is interesting is that suicide as portrayed in the movies, which is common, is depicted as a social act, caused by social factors, the most predominant one being relationship strain (Stack & Bowman, 2012). Some researchers and clinicians have been questioning this individual and pathological stance of suicidology, wanting to expand into qualitative and ethnographic research, into understanding suicide from the person's or a community's point of view, seeing suicide from a cultural vantage point, and seeing suicide prevention from different angles such as being community-driven (Kral & Idlout, 2016). A new field of critical suicidology is emerging, questioning the status quo and providing new, innovative, and alternative perspectives on suicide and its prevention (White, Marsh, Kral, & Morris, 2016). This critical stance is not to replace the traditional work in suicidology, but to expand it. My book will fit into this new critical suicidology. My book will not be about suicide in different cultures per se, although I will present and discuss this. This book is anthropological, but also psychological. It is about how individuals internalize culture, how the mind and culture are constituted of each other. Suicide is seen as a social disorder. My book will fit with the newer look in anthropology on cultural transmission and the propagation of ideas (Bloch, 2005; Bentley, Earls, & O'Brien, 2011; Schönpflug, 2009a). We will better understand how suicide becomes an acceptable option by examining and studying the phenomenon of the idea. We need to learn more about how ideas are adopted more generally in the first place, how they are spread throughout society, and how they change over time.

Culture

The concept of culture should first be examined. What is culture? In anthropology the term has produced much debate. Burke (2005, p. 119) notes that the concept of culture has "an embarrassing variety of definitions." The ambiguity of the culture concept has not been resolved (Stocking, 1992a). Shore (1996, p. 8) writes about anthropology's use of culture, noting that "the concept of culture, long the defining idea of our discipline, is in deep trouble." He notes that culture in anthropology has many meanings:

> A patchwork of traits, integrated configurations, constellations of symbols and meanings, symbolic templates, a web of meanings, taxonomic trees, measurable units of behavior, a collection of material artifacts, systems of knowledge, sets of values and beliefs, sets of characteristic strategies for accomplishing a desired goal, and, more recently, a field on which a cacophonous cluster of diverse voices or "discourses" plays itself out.

He sees culture as "a very large and heterogeneous collection of *models* or what psychologists sometimes call schemas" (p. 44). These are knowledge structures (Casson, 1983). Schemas are developed in cultural contexts (Cerulo, 2002). Nishida (2005, pp. 402, 404) defines cultural schemas as "generalized collections of the knowledge that we store in memory through experiences in our own culture," "a stock of knowledge of appropriate behavior and an appropriate role he or she should play in the situation." Cultural schemas organize and process experience, and some anthropologists see cultural models as larger and more complex (Quinn, 2011). Bloch (2012) finds great similarity in the concepts of scripts, schemas, mental models, and cultural models. A schema is a memory structure (Derry, 1996). Schemas can have motivational properties and can organize desirable or undesirable states of mind (Horowitz & Stinson, 1995). Kroeber and Kluckhohn (1952) reviewed the various definitions of culture. They found 164 different definitions and wrote that "culture is an abstract description of *trends toward* uniformity in the words, acts, and artifacts of human groups" (in original) (p. 359). They cited the coming of the culture concept "as the foundation stone in the social sciences," with the idea of culture being "one of the key notions of contemporary American thought" (Kroeber & Kluckhohn, 1952, p. 3). The authors provided the following definition: "Culture consists of patterns, explicit and implicit, of and for behavior acquired and transmitted by symbols, constituting the distinctive achievement of human groups, including their embodiments in artifacts; the essential core of culture consists of traditional (i.e., historically derived and selected) ideas and especially their attached values; culture systems may on the one hand be considered as products of action, on the other as conditioning elements of further action" (p. 357). Ross (2004, p. 68) has culture as shared meanings, as "the distribution of knowledge, ideas, and values." For Bloch (2012, p. 33), culture is "the process of transmission through communication." Culture can be essentialized, ignoring within-group differences and assuming that everyone is thinking the same way. Culture is, rather, a moving process. Biologist Richard Dawkins (2016, p. 4), author of *The Selfish Gene*, writes, "Some would say that culture is so important that genes, whether selfish or not, are virtually irrelevant to the understanding of human nature."

Geertz (1973, p. 5) has culture as "webs of significance people have themselves spun," where "I take culture to be those webs, and the analysis of it to be therefore not an experimental science in search of law but an interpretive one in search of meaning." Culture for Geertz is public because meaning is, and it is ideational. "Culture consists of socially established structures of meaning" (p. 12), "Cultural systems must have a minimal degree of coherence, [or] else we would not call them systems" (p. 17). "Cultural analysis is intrinsically incomplete. And, worse than that, the more deeply it goes the less complete it is" (p. 29). Culture for Geertz was a combination of core symbols, underlying structures, and ideologies. It was about knowing how people understand themselves (Rosaldo, 1999). Culture is indeed a shared meaning system, what people have in common, and even how people see themselves. Harari (2011) believes that cultures are the diversity of imagined realities, what he calls mythical glue, and that people are born into pre-existing imagined orders shaped by a culture's dominant myths. Cultures "create imagined orders and devised scripts" (p. 149), an "intersubjective reality ıt exists solely in people's shared imagination" (p. 197). Even though their culture has changed significantly, the Inuit in Arctic Canada I have worked with for over 20 years still see themselves as having a culture that is different from mainstream Canadian culture. This is referred to as cultural identity. Oyserman and Lee (2007, p. 272) write that "culture matters, influencing how the self is defined, how relationships with others are imagined, what is of value and worth, and how the mind works." Tolman (1998) corrected Descartes with *sumus ergo sum*, we are therefore I am, rather than *cogito ergo sum* (I think therefore I am), seeing the person becoming a person in a public space. As Floyd Allport (1924, p. 325) wrote some time ago, "My idea of myself is thus largely my neighbor's idea of me, or rather my own idea of my neighbor's idea of me." In 1895, Le Bon wrote about crowds, which he believed were unconscious and prone to "contagious suggestion" (Le Bon, 1960/1895, p. 41). He argued that emotions are contagious, and "Contagion is so powerful that it forces upon individuals not only certain opinions, but certain modes of feeling as well" (p. 128), and "Man, like animals, has a natural tendency to imitation" (p. 127).

The diversity of "imagined realities" resulting in the diversity of behavior, as well as the myths and fictions we learn from birth on, thinking in certain ways, learning certain rules of life, are fundamental aspects of culture (Harari, 2011, p. 41). Psychological processes are constituted by culture (Richardson & Fowers, 2010). Indeed, culture mediates our existence (Teo, 2017). Culture, according to Sperber (1996a), is made up of contagious ideas. To explain culture, he argues, is to explain how some ideas become contagious. He calls this the epidemiology of representations, the distribution of mental states in a population (Droit & Sperber, 1999). This is after Durkheim's notion of collective representations. What is linked are the public and the mental, again the co-constitution of culture and mind. Markus and Hamedani (2007, pp. 4–5) note that "as people actively construct their worlds, they are made up of, or 'constituted by,' relations with other people and by the ideas, practices, products, and institutions that are prevalent in their social contexts (i.e., environments, fields, situations, settings, worlds). . . . Individuals are ineluctably social and cultural phenomena." Some cultural representations in the mind are useful, and others are harmful. Very similar representations are distributed in a population. Representations are internalized psychologically, and internalization will be described in detail in Chapter 4. The self is culturally shaped, as seen in comparisons between North American and Asian people (Kitayama, Duffy, & Uchida, 2007). Culture affects emotions (Anderson, 2011; Mesquita & Leu, 2007), moral development (Miller, 2007; Shweder, Mahapatra, & Miller, 1990), social identity, (Brewer & Yuki, 2007), and memory (Bloch, 2012; Wang & Ross, 2007), and it is critical in shaping the onset, experience, expression, course, and outcome of mental disorders (Marsella & Yamada, 2007). Culture even shapes our posture and stance (Mead, 1972). Culture shapes how we *r*elop as children (Berry, Poortinga, Segall, & Dasen, 1992; Gardiner, 01). It shapes how we think (Goodnow, 1990; Kashima, 2001; Nis-_ tt, 2003), how we are motivated to do things (D'Andrade & Strauss, 1992; Munro, Schumaker, & Carr, 1997), and how identity and the self exist (Allen, 1997; Markus, Mullally, & Kitayama, 1997). The self is seen as social, as relational (Gergen, 2011). Fivush and Buckner (1997) see the self itself as a social-cultural process. Martin and Sugarman (1999, p. 32) see that

> selves need societies, just as societies need selves. A psychological being develops a self only because it is part of a community of other selves, past and present, that has constructed a public, social world of common symbols, systems, and practices capable of underwriting a pattern of interactions in which selves influence and respond to other selves.

Suicide Contagion

Rather that treating suicide contagion and clusters as a form of (tragic) error variance, to use statistical language, I believe that the social and cultural influence on suicide should be seen as a main effect. It tells us a great deal about the phenomenon of suicide. To be sure, the media reporting prevention efforts by the CDC and others are to be commended (Pirkis, Blood, Beautrais, Burgess, & Skehan, 2006). But they actually get at the heart of the matter, that suicide is a socially contagious phenomenon in general. Human meaning is collective (Baumeister & Landau, 2018). The meaning of suicide is thus collective, spread socially. Suicide can be "normalized" by the media and other sources (SAMHSA, 2017). Chu, Goldblum, Floyd, and Bongar (2010) write about attitudes they call cultural sanctions, and they add that culture contributes to suicide through the suicidal behavior of close others and one's own attitudes and behavior concerning suicide. Suicide by cluster and contagion may be at the center of understanding this phenomenon. Cheng et al. (2014) found 340 academic articles on suicide contagion between 1960 and 2013, so there has been much interest in this phenomenon. Exposure to suicides of others increases one's likelihood of being suicidal (Swanson & Colman, 2013). Even biologically oriented suicidologists mention the imitative and contagious aspect of suicide (e.g., Jamison, 1999), yet it remains to be theorized within the field.

In my theory of suicide, presented in Chapter 4, suicide is seen as a function of two factors: perturbation and lethality. Perturbation means being upset, anxious, depressed, irritated, shaken, angry, guilty, shamed, and so on. Lethality in my view is the idea of suicide, the idea of death to stop the perturbation. This book is about a lethality theory of suicide. Lethality is the killer. It is the intentionality and singularity of suicide as an option to end perturbation. It involves selecting the permanent cessation of consciousness as the escape plan. It is the adoption of suicide as an idea, as a plan of action. Perturbation does not cause suicide, although most suicidologists think it does. Crossing one's threshold of tolerance for perturbation is usually believed to be the most important precursor to suicide (Menninger, 1938; Motto, 1992). Perturbation acts as motivation when a threshold of tolerance is crossed. It is argued here that perturbation can never be more than an *indirect* cause of suicide. It causes us to do something about the perturbation. While we have learned much about perturbation, we still know little about lethality. And where do we get most of our ideas? We get them from our cultural surround. We get them from other people. It is my view, based on the early theory of sociologist Gabriel Tarde (1903, 1904), that the sharing of ideas is how culture works. We imitate each other; we imitate role models. The second factor in the theory is that suicide is an idea internalized from culture. Imitation is a form of cultural learning. Tomasello, Kruger, and Ratner (1993, p. 497) see imitative learning as "the learner internalizes something of the demonstrator's behavioral strategies." Infants imitate already when they are a few hours old (Meltzoff & Moore, 1977, 1983). We grow up in a culture where we internalize almost everything we do, and even who we are. We are socially constructed (Gergen, 1999, 2001). We acquire ideas about suicide from our culture. As Hacking (1999) writes, ideas "inhabit a social setting" (p. 10). The reasons for and of suicide vary widely around the world, yet are shared by people living close to each other. Anthropologists have long noted difference in suicide methods across societies, sometimes being quite "stereotyped and distinctive" (La Fontaine, 1975, p. 81). Suicide is culturally scripted; it becomes a cultural idiom of distress that for some can become a normative option (Nichter, 2010). Winterrowd, Canetto, and Benoit (2015) found that suicide among the elderly in America is culturally acceptable because of physical illness, and this attitude becomes a cultural script for suicide among the elderly.

Servitje and Nixon (2016) find that contagion is endemic to contemporary culture and has been part of human history for centuries. There is now even a neurobiology of imitation in mirror neurons, a system that understands actions of others and replicates those actions, neurons that fire when an action is seen and also performed (Iacoboni et al., 1999; Rizzolatti, 2005; Wohlschlager & Bekkering, 2002). The mirror neuron system is about understanding actions performed by others (Rizzolatti, 2005). Neuronal "activity is triggered not only by the observation of an action but also by the sound produced by that action. . . . This otherness with which we are saturated and that constitutes us is the human condition" (Oughourlian, 2016, pp. 27, 45). The other becomes a model. Ideas are out there in public in social settings. Ideas can become normative. Norms are both ideational and behavioral, as in behavioral regularities seen collectively as appropriate. Norms can be internalized and become an "oughtness," something that should be done. Some norms are more accepted than others. Norms are more likely to be internalized if they are ambiguous or vague, allowing for flexibility in choice (Hechter & Opp, 2001). As Wedenoja and Sobo (1997, p. 162) state, "Culture is knowledge that is shared or public . . . virtually everything we think or do involves culture." Imitation is important for an understanding of the ecology of human cognition and norms, the mutual influence of cognition and culture (Hurley & Chater, 2005b). The effects of imitation can be seen in Bourdieu's concept of habitus, which is a set of dispositions, knowledge, and understandings of the world, that is created through socialization (Mahar, Harker, & Wilkes, 1990). Even O'Dea (1882) over a century ago thought that suicide was imitated.

Bandura (2001) has discussed social learning theory and social diffusion. This theory sees people as agentic, as self-organizing, proactive, and self-regulating, and has the proposition that we learn social behavior by observing and imitating. People can direct themselves. They model their behavior after others, and this modeling is furthered through the mass media. They are motivated by people similar to themselves, and modeling strongly influences motivation. Emotions increase observation of others. Copying others is increased by seeing the benefits of the action. For suicide, people do choose to internalize and copy the thoughts and behavior of suicidal others, and are motivated by seeing that suicide does end perturbation and has a desired effect. In their theory of crime as choice, Wilson and Herrnstein (1985, p. 43) note that at the center of their theory is the assumption that "people, when faced with a choice, choose the preferred course of action. . . . A person will do that thing the consequences of which are perceived by him or her to be preferable to the consequences of doing something else." People choose suicide; it is an idea they have accepted and selected as a choice. Certain groups are more affected by contagion than others, which can be called fads (Meyersohn & Katz, 1957).

Contagion can also be referred to as herd behavior or informational cascades (Bikhchandani, Hirshleifer, & Welch, 1992; Gale, 1996). Reviewing the research on diffusion, Strang and Soule (1998) see diffusion as the spread of something within a social system. They show how cultural models condition behavior, and that the mass media is greatly influential. Marshall McLuhan believed the media manipulated people (Gordon, 1997). Internal diffusion is the flow of information within a particular group. Smith (1933, p. 10) wrote about diffusion that the borrowed ideas become integrated into the receiver's personality and more or less modified in the process of adaptation to his or her knowledge and interests." People have agency while also being socially influenced, as having a self-consciously interpretive system in place when adopting or internalizing new information. Writing about why ideas "stick" in people's heads,

Heath and Heath (2007) believe that ideas need to be simple, unexpected, concrete, credible, and narrative, and they should elicit emotions.

Ideas and behaviors can be imitated through cultural transmission. Berry and Georgas (2009) describe three forms of such transmission as vertical, horizontal, and oblique. Vertical transmission is cultural values, skills, beliefs, and motives passed on by parents to their children. Trommsdorff (2009, p. 129) showed a model of internalization where "the child actively participates in the socialization process by interpreting, evaluating, either accepting or rejecting the parents' message, and, finally, possibly conforming and internalizing the message, thus matching their own intentions with those of their parents." Furthermore, the child's behavior influences the way the parents interact with the child. So here the socialization is bidirectional. The values transmitted may be morals, life goals, violence, social prejudices, stereotypes, political orientations; they can be many things. Horizontal transmission comes from one's peers, and oblique transmission from social institutions. Such social learning has the person see things from the other person's perspective. Empathy encourages imitation (Iacoboni, 2005). Hebb (1980, p. 25) cites Köhler (1927) showing that even chimpanzees imitate each other:

> The second animal, whose task is to reach a banana hung high up, stands on a precarious structure of boxes piled on one another and stretches for the prize now barely with reach; at which point the first animal, who has already solved the problem and is now made to sit to one side and look on, reaches upward with his arm at the same time and in the same posture. His idea, his expectation, of the other's action produces the same action in himself.

This is the work of mirror neurons.

Again, researchers have found that imitation is a critical form of social learning from infancy onward (Meltzoff, 2011; Miller & Dollard, 1941; Nadel & Butterworth, 1999; Nielsen & Slaughter, 2007). Imitative learning is the first form of cultural learning (Tomasello, 1999). Newborns at 32 hours old can imitate facial acts, as found by Meltzoff (2005). He found 12- to 21-day-olds were able to imitate tongue protrusion, and indicates studies have found infants to be able to copy mouth opening, hand movements, emotional expressions, head movements, lip and cheek movements, and eye blinking. Newborns thus imitate facial acts they have never done. But infants cannot imitate the way older children do. "The ability of young infants to interpret the bodily acts of others in terms of their own acts and experiences gives them a tool for cracking the problem of other minds. . . . Infants may use their own intentional actions as a framework for interpreting the intentional actions of others" (Meltzoff, 2005, p. 75). Jones (2007), on the other hand, did not find 6-month-old infants to be able to mimic, or reproduce another person's specific muscle movements. She concluded that the ability to imitate specific motor acts takes most of the first two years of life to develop. Anisfeld (2005) reports that the ability to imitate disappears after the first weeks of life and returns at about 6 or 9 months of age. Nielsen and Slaughter (2007) indicate that infants also learn deferred imitation, which is the infant's capacity to imitate a model right away and then later. This is seen in infants as young as 6 to 9 months of age. We continue to imitate throughout life. Donald (2005, p. 298) writes, "Accurate imitation is so highly developed in humans that it stands out as one of the defining characteristics of the human mind." Research supports that imitation is thus central to human development, the ability to understand other minds, language, relationships, and social life in general (Berger, 2013; Hurley & Chater, 2005a; Nehaniv & Dautenhahn, 2007). Yet very young children do have innate predispositions that allow them to master many tasks (Bloch, 2012). As Pinker (2012, p. 60) states, "Culture relies on neural circuitry that accomplishes the feat we call learning." Yet we are social animals and develop as such. Martin and Sugarman (2003, p. 83) state that "caregivers and others interact with the infant in ways that furnish the developing infant with the various practices, forms, and means of personhood and identity extant within the particular society and culture within which the infant exists. Psychological development now proceeds as the internalization and appropriation of sociocultural practices as psychological tools, that is, vehicles for language and thought."

Book Structure

Chapter 2 examines theories of suicide. Here I also examine how suicide has been viewed over time. Suicide is the act of willfully taking one's own life. Chapter 3 is about social epidemics. Human imitation has sometimes been taken on by many people in one setting. People in large groups can copy each other, and again this is how culture works. Mass hysteria is a form of collective imitation. Albert Camus (1955, p. 3) famously wrote that there is "but one truly serious philosophical problem, and that is suicide." Looking at suicide has increasingly occupied the work of historians. Writers on the subject have long noted changes over time, often dramatic ones, in public attitudes toward suicide. Depending on the era and the context, suicide has been viewed in a number of different ways. One prominent polarity concerning how suicide has been viewed, which still registers occasional debate today, is that of free will versus determinism. As a problem, suicide has been discussed, debated, vilified, outlawed, prescribed, legalized, and studied over a great period of time. Yet suicide remains an enigma. Given the riddle of suicide, multiple frames have been used and constructed in order that this phenomenon might be explained or understood. In Chapter 2 I attempt an organization of some of the primary frames through which suicide has been viewed. I review the main historical, biological, psychological, psychiatric, sociological, and cultural anthropological approaches to suicide. Again, the most common approach to suicide has been through the disciplines of psychology and psychiatry, seeing suicide as a result of a mental disorder like depression or an accumulation of risk factors such has hopelessness, lack of belonging, perceived burdensomeness, problem-solving deficits, guilt, and so on. This is a deterministic way of seeing suicide, as caused by some internal or external factors rather than being the free will of the person. I will explore this debate about free will versus determinism in suicide.

In Chapter 4, culture and suicide will be examined. Anthropology has been the least explored frame toward suicide, and I argue that it may in fact be the most illuminating regarding our understanding of this phenomenon. I attempt to link anthropology with psychology in the process, given that suicide is both a collective and an individual behavior. I outline the beginning of a cultural-psychological model I see as critical to furthering our understanding of suicide, one that I have written about (Kral, 1994, 1998). This chapter will outline how lethality or the idea of suicide is learned through culture, of how suicide is imitated and how it is contagious. I will also examine how suicide differs across cultures.

In Chapter 5 I will look more closely at the theory of cultural imitation by Gabriel Tarde. Invention or agency is the "very texture" of the process of imitation, working not from the outside in, which Durkheim argued, but from the inside out (Karsenti, 2010, p. 59). Martin, Sugarman, and Thompson (2003) see agency as embedded and situated, situated in historical sociocultural contexts. For Tarde, personality and culture were intertwined. Beliefs and desires were psychological characteristics essential for imitation. Tarde also emphasized agency with his focus on invention, conscious volition, the source of human innovation and progress. There are also suicide epidemics. In the 1970s and 1980s on the South Pacific Islands of Micronesia, there was a teenage suicide epidemic where the suicide rate was 10 times higher than in other places in the world, and the teenagers were killing themselves in the same way under the same circumstances (Gladwell, 2000). Coleman (2004) has written about copycat suicides, much of it inspired by the media. Starting in 2002, a shooting spree happened in the U.S. where at least 13 people were shot, and ten were killed. The next month, three sniper incidents took place, and three more took place the month after that. After 9/11, there were a number of planes crashing into buildings as murder-suicides.

The Emergence of Critical Suicidology

The view of suicide from a cultural vantage point in this book fits with a critical suicidology or critical suicide studies. Critical suicidology moves beyond this narrow perspective and methodology to open up new ways of thinking about suicide and suicide prevention. It is more contextualized, ethnographic and qualitative, subjective, historical, ecological, political, and focused on social justice. The subjective side includes experiences of those who have attempted suicide or who have been suicidal. Critical suicidology can even be poetic (Jaworski & Scott, 2016). It is a reframing of suicidology.

Papers have been published on critical suicidology in a recent book (White et al., 2016) and a special issue of the journal *Death Studies* (Kral & White, 2017). They will be summarized here to give the reader a flavor of what this new field looks like. There have also been three conferences on critical suicidology in 2016 and 2017 in Prague, the Czech Republic, and Canterbury, England, and in 2018 in Perth, Australia. The scholars attending this conference are international, from many different countries including Sweden, Denmark, Ghana, South Africa, Australia, Canada, the U.S., England, the Czech Republic, and Poland. There is much interest in the critical suicidology endeavor.

Beginning with critical suicidology, White et al. (2016, p. 3) write that "when a singular form of evidence is privileged as superior or more 'truthful' than others, much gets lost, including creativity, plurality, and freedom of thought." Ian Marsh (2016) begins with a critique of mainstream suicidology. Mainstream suicidology sees suicide as pathological and individual, and sees itself as a science. Suicide has been pathological since its medicalization (MacDonald, 1989). The science of suicide is primarily through quantitative research, which while it has taught us much about suicide, it is limited with a need for a wider lens of investigation (Hjelmeland & Knizek, 2010). Seen as the result of an individual, the social in suicide is left out. Yet suicide can be seen as a social act.

In reviewing the three main journals in suicidology, Heidi Hjelmeland (2016) finds that most of the studies are on risk factors for suicide, and the vast majority of suicide research is conducted in the U.S. She believes that suicide research should be from other countries and cultural contexts. I believe that risk factors are related much more to perturbation than to suicide. These are reasons people are upset. Hjelmeland also finds suicidology to be atheoretical. She calls for qualitative research on suicide, and that this should be encouraged by the editors of suicide journals. Also needed are cultural studies on suicide, which we have seen is just beginning.

Wexler and Gone (2016) offer a view of suicide prevention for Indigenous peoples. They note that the individual focus of suicidology does not fit with the Indigenous view of the person as relational. Intervention is directed at mental health rather than social factors, and through health systems rather than community projects. They argue that Indigenous suicide prevention "must be formulated in response to local Indigenous meanings and practices" rather than being an extension of colonialism.

Indigenous best practices for suicide prevention are described by Kral and Idlout (2016). They take a historical and cultural approach to Inuit suicide in the Canadian Arctic. Historically, Inuit were visited by explorers in the 1500s–1700s, by whalers in the late nineteenth and early twentieth centuries, and by missionaries, the police, and fur traders from the 1920s to the 1950s. Then the grand colonial work began by the Canadian government in the late 1950s. This has been called the government era, where Inuit were moved from their family-based land camps to crowded settlements run by a White government worker, children were taken away and sent to boarding/residential or day schools, a cash economy was established with few jobs that created poverty, gender roles were changed especially for men, and Inuit became dependent on the settlement. The most negative effect of this colonialism/imperialism was on family and interpersonal relations. As a collectivist, family-based culture, when the family is dramatically changed, everything will go wrong. When the children of the boarding/residential and day schools grew up, they began having problems with alcohol and domestic violence. Their children started killing themselves in the mid-1980s. They now have one of the highest suicide rates in the world, all young people. When I began studying suicide among the Inuit, my team and I discovered that one community had done something themselves and the suicides stopped for about five years. In another community that was participating in the research, a local youth organization opened a youth center for suicide prevention and the suicides stopped for a few years. Then the suicides returned after it was closed, and a next generation of youth re-opened it. In the eight years after they opened it compared to the eight years previous, suicides decreased by 68%. Kral and Idlout argue that suicide prevention should be community-driven, and each community should decide what to do. They show that the Canadian government now has an Indigenous youth suicide prevention policy where they fund communities to develop and run their own suicide prevention programs (Kral et al., 2009). There is no prescribed approach to suicide prevention. What makes these programs work is that they are owned by the communities.

Jonny Morris (2016) writes as an educator about suicide and suicide prevention among youth. The school-based suicide prevention programs in the 1980s were primarily based on a stress model of suicide, seeing suicide as caused by stress that could happen to anyone, and Morris notes that in more recent years suicide prevention uses a mental illness model of suicide. Morris describes his own research on school-based suicide prevention and on how suicide is constructed through discourses in the classroom. He found that educators are seen as "truth-tellers" who do not listen to the knowledge of the young people participating in the program. He believes that such programs should recruit young people as consultants, seeing suicide prevention from their point of view. They are the experts on their own lives.

Like Jonny Morris, Jennifer White (2016) writes about school-based suicide prevention. She uses a critical constructionist framework emphasizing social justice and transformation, youth participation, and social constructionism. White reviews the limitations of conventional ways of thinking about youth suicide prevention and research. She indicates some unspoken assumptions in youth suicide awareness programs, such as seeing students as fragile or ill, as discredited, and as passive. She has an alternative construction of youth, one that focuses on local youth participation and addresses social, cultural, economic, and political factors, including social justice oriented approaches. White wishes to promote conversation and youth leadership in suicide prevention, a democratizing angle seeing students as experts.

Fullagar and O'Brien (2016) examine suicide attempts and recovery within women's narratives of depression in Australia. They conducted a qualitative study with 80 women and analyzed the gendered context of suicide and these women's identities, relationships, and emotional subjectivities. The women's suicidal feelings were connected to their relationships, with the paradox of caring for others, which depleted them emotionally. Many felt that they failed at caring for others. The authors believe that gendered inequities are part of these women's emotional distress through their relationships.

Narrative practices are also discussed by Sather and Newman (2016). They present a study they conducted where they collected stories about how people cope with the suicide of a loved one, from six different countries including Nigeria and New Zealand. They were interested in "first person" accounts. The participants they interviewed were very grateful for being able to speak about the suicides. They thought it was a way of honoring the person who died. The paper is primarily about the stories themselves, as presented by the participants. This first person telling is another way of educating the reader, rather than reviewing the literature or presenting quantitative data on risk factors.

Bergmans, Rowe, Dineen, and Johnson (2016) are two social workers and two people who have attempted suicide. They are each other's teachers and students, and give examples of their lived experiences of being suicidal and working with suicidal people. Bergmans reports a few suicide attempt referrals to her program, where the person doing the referring stereotyped, used biomedical language, and sounded objectivist. There is minimization of the distress, reductionism, and distancing from the patient. Dineen indicates that his doctor used the term borderline to keep describing him and what he should be experiencing, without hearing his voice. The authors call for hearing the suicidal person's experience and for collaboration with patients, which can strengthen the sense of safety and increase confidence. They show that research supports the efficacy with suicidal people of a strong client–care provider alliance.

Andrea Rowe (2016) describes her lived experience with recurrent suicidality, and the social and medical stigma associated with suicidal people. Over 15 years she has had 20 to 30 psychiatric hospitalizations. As she writes, "I have begun to deconstruct my pathology, detaching myself from my complete reliance on a medical model of care in which the patient is essentially passive and receives care, toward a more active participatory engagement in meaning making" (p. 155). She accepted responsibility for transforming her life. She has become a researcher, an academic, a humanitarian, a social worker, a peer support worker, and an advocate for speaking out against stigmas "that label sufferers like myself as somehow 'defective,' 'less-than,' or 'black sheep'" (p. 163). She practices mindfulness and yoga, and today has no regrets. She is able to connect with others who have had similar experiences as her. This is a story of how one person managed to free herself of the pain that made her suicidal.

Rob Cover (2016) looks at queer youth suicide, as LGBT people are at higher risk for suicidal ideation, suicide attempts, and suicide. He shows how the media, through film and television, portray LGBT people as sad, self-hating, shamed, isolated, and rejected. Suicidology uses a pathologizing psychiatric approach to queer youth suicide. All representations create a major difference between heterosexual and non-heterosexual youth. Yet social stressors are deemed to also be responsible for their suicidality. Cover looks at the suicidal sexual subject as a cultural and historical product, addressing the formation of sexual identity. He demonstrates that poststructural and queer theory are absent in research on queer suicide. Queer suicide is based in shame over non-normativity and a failure to meet cultural expectations.

Jaworski and Scott (2016) write about how suicide remains unfathomable in everyday life, and how poetry signifies our understanding of suicide, our ability to see suicide's unfathomability. With suicide taking place in a private space, it is absent when it takes place. Absence has suicide as an ethical gift, putting a mark on our own time lines. The authors provide three poems that they then analyze. The first sees suicide as a rupture, "a tear in the time of one's life" (p. 214). The psychache of the suicide is transferred to the survivors. The second poem asks "why" about suicide, about the suicide rejecting others. It places suicide as dependent on what we do not know, and suicide is never accessible. The third poem returns to absence and shows that there is no end to grieving suicide. Survivors cannot forget. That suicide is impossible to understand has it remaining unresolved. The authors conclude that "poetry's role is to acknowledge not only the ineffable acceptance of death but also an acceptance that our lives and deaths are not entirely up to us. Perhaps we, as human beings, are undone from the beginning and know it only when it is too late" (p. 225).

The special issue of the journal *Death Studies* includes a poem by the journal's editor Robert Neimeyer. Poetry can indeed help us understand suicide. Jennifer White (2017), a co-editor with me of this special issue, has a paper where she asks, "What can critical psychology do?" She presents the mainstream approach in suicidology:

> Authoritative knowledge about suicide is produced through scientific research; this leads to the construction of suicide as a particular kind of problem that can be acted upon; this knowledge is then 'applied' to practice; and the goal of preventing and controlling suicide in the population is expected to follow.
>
> (p. 472)

White sees suicide through a lens of relational entanglements, and critical suicidology as working through ongoing tensions, fragmented understandings, and contradictions. Suicide is not to be simplified, and its complexity needs much exploration. Suicide is a social act. She suggests that suicidal ideation be seen as a life-activating practice, that we should engage with the paradoxes in life and death, and that suicide should be re-conceptualized as a political issue.

Hjelmeland and Knizek (2017) argue against the common belief that over 90% of suicides have had a mental disorder. They show that the mental disorder belief is guided by idealogy, politics, power, and vested interest among professionals. The mental disorder notion is based on psychological autopsy studies, where family and friends of the diseased are interviewed. One cannot diagnose someone by interviewing someone else. How would someone else know whether the person had all the symptoms of a particular mental disorder? This is impossible. Diagnosis by proxy is invalid. The authors claim that those supporting the 90% statistic find people like them to have "unsubstantiated opinions." They cite one author whose abstract on critical suicidology was rejected from a suicide conference as being "a political speech." The belief that mental disorders cause suicide is wrong. Some mental disorders are associated with suicide, as these people are vulnerable to the idea of suicide. As mentioned earlier in this book, mental disorders are forms of perturbation. They do not "cause" anything. What one does about this perturbation is, again, open.

Galasinski and Ziolkowska (2017) present a study they conducted in Poland on the construction of suicidal ideation in medical records, how patients' stories are transformed into medical discourses. Medical records document diagnostic and therapeutic processes and all communication with the patient, the patient's family, and other clinicians. In this study the authors explored the sources of constructions of suicidal ideation in medical records, and examined the relationship between patients' accounts of suicidal ideation and what was written in the record. They compared recordings of psychiatric interviews with what was written. The authors found that the experiences of the patients were ignored in the records, as were the social contexts. Suicidal ideation was constructed as an objective phenomenon, as an all or nothing reality.

Colucci, Too, and Minas (2017) write about another study, one conducted in Australia. This was with immigrant and refugee populations, who are at higher risk for suicide. Participants ranked the importance of a set of research questions about mental health, and they included people with lived experience of suicidal behaviors and professionals. They then responded to another set of questions. They found low rates of access to mental health services by immigrants and refugees, and participants felt that more research was needed on suicidal behavior among these groups. The authors presented the priorities that participants evaluated for mental health, which included looking at barriers to access and engagement in suicide prevention services, protective factors, culturally appropriate risk assessment, key risk factors, prevalence of suicidal behavior, and cultural values and beliefs about suicide.

Bantes and Swartz (2017) write about their qualitative research with traditional healers in South Africa. They interviewed traditional healers about their understanding of suicidal behavior and how they respond to suicidal individuals. The healers indicated that they were frequently consulted by people with suicidal thoughts. They took their time and listened carefully to these people. Interventions included helping the person reconnect with ancestors, washing the person with herbs and using traditional medicine, and prescribing rituals such as travel. Other interventions were similar to Western ones, including empathic listening.

Osafo, Akotia, Hjeleland, and Knizek (2017) conducted a qualitative study in Ghana on attitudes toward suicide. A suicide attempt in Ghana is against the law. The authors found two views of suicide that are prevalent: suicide as moral transgression and suicide as life crisis. The life crisis view is held primarily by health and mental health professionals. This includes unemployment, social taunting, academic stress, hopelessness, fear of shame, interpersonal tensions, neglect, faith crisis, and other general existential struggles. It also includes mental disorders. The moral transgression view sees suicide as an affront to self-love and neighbor love. This moral view is widespread among rural and urban people, and represents a cultural meaning of suicide. The suicidal person is viewed as antisocial, a sinner, and a criminal. Suicide stigma is shared and is seen at the family, community, legal, and religious levels. The moral view also sees the person as sane and capable of intentionality.

Polanco, Mancias, and LeFeber (2017) write about their development of a qualitative study, which they call an interpretive phenomenological analysis. They examine what prevented U.S. Military service members from taking their life when they attempted to do so. Suicide is the primary cause of death among active duty military service members during times of peace. In this study the authors used a strengths-based perspective, focusing on social, relational, and historical resources as opposed to risk factors.

Finally, Colin Tatz (2017) is conducting research on the criteria cor-
ners use in determining suicide as a cause of death. He finds under-
reporting of suicide to be a serious problem. This may be especially so
in rural areas and where suicide is stigmatized. In New Zealand it has been
reported that the suicide rate is likely 3 times the rate reported. Tatz has
worked in particular with the Australian Aboriginal population, which
has a very high suicide rate. Colonization of these people was severe and
included episodic killing between 1804 and 1928. Up to the 1980s they
had no civil or civic rights and there was much child removal, called "the
stolen generation." They were wards of the state. They suffered a trauma
Durkheim called anomie, or "a condition in which society provides little
moral guidance to individuals" (Gerber & Macionis, 2010). Tatz notes
that suicide is still not talked about, that principals in Australia's schools
refuse to have suicide become a topic of discussion. "The entire cultural
and historical complexity of suicide needs to be opened to discussion,
even confrontation" (p. 14).

Critical suicidology is thus about new ideas, new visions. Going
beyond suicide caused by mental disorders, looking at Indigenous suicide
prevention through Indigenous eyes, involving youth in youth suicide
prevention, hearing the experiences of those who have been suicidal,
understanding suicide through poetry, seeing community-driven rather
than "evidence based" suicide prevention, looking at Indigenous traditional healing, are all examples of critical suicidology. This book on a
cultural theory of suicide is also critical suicidology. Culture needs to be
brought into suicidology and suicide needs to be understood as cultural. It
can be a cultural idiom of distress for vulnerable, perturbed people. It is
about the mind and culture coming together. Humans are cultural animals
to their core.

This book examines suicide from the wide lens of culture. We will see
how imitative humans are of each other, how cultural models are internalized, and how cultural ideas can even become epidemics of mass hysteria. Different frames of suicide have been described, and all are valid.
An anthropological-psychological model of suicide is presented as the
combination of perturbation and lethality, where lethality is the idea of
suicide. The cultural theory of Gabriel Tarde is explored as a way of
looking at suicide, as imitation and contagion. Suicide should be seen
the way we see other human acts, as something learned from culture. The
idea of suicide is the reason people kill themselves. Suicide becomes the
choice taken. In 1998 I proposed three questions for suicidology: (1) How
deeply embedded is suicide in the cultural system of ideas? (2) Who is
more prone to internalize the idea of suicide, and under what personal
and cultural conditions? (3) Is it time to ask different questions in suicidology? (Kral, 1998).

2 On Suicide

Culture has been little integrated into suicidology (Colucci & Lester, 2013; Munster & Broz, 2015; White et al., 2016), with the mainstream view seeing suicide as an individual act. Freud (1917, p. 252) referred to suicide as a riddle, not being able to understand how a being could destroy itself. He theorized that we don't actually kill our self, but a symbolic representation of somebody else we both love and hate who we wish was dead. There has been an enormous amount of research and writing on suicide since Durkheim's famous book on suicide in 1897, yet it still remains a mystery. We have learned of numerous risk factors for suicide, from being male to being depressed, abusing substances, being gay, being hopeless, feeling like you don't belong, in general being very perturbed, but none of these things leads directly to suicide. They lead to being upset. Most people with all these suicide risk factors will never kill themselves. What leads someone to make the decision to kill himself or herself? Where does the idea of suicide come from?

Seeing Suicide: Conceptual Frames

Given the riddle of suicide, multiple frames have been used and constructed in order that this phenomenon might be explained or understood. In this chapter I attempt an organization of some of the primary frames through which suicide has been viewed. I review the main historical, biological, psychological, sociological, and cultural anthropological approaches to suicide. Emphasis is on the cultural from a Durkheimian and Tardeian angle. In Chapter 4 I outline the beginning of a cultural-psychological model I see as critical to furthering our understanding of suicide.

A brief definition of suicide is in order at the outset of this chapter. On the surface, perhaps the most common definition of suicide is the voluntary taking of one's own life. The problem arises immediately with the word *voluntary*, however. There is currently a move, one might say a politically correct one, to end the use of the phrase "to *commit* suicide," so that causal attributions may be ascribed to conditions beyond the person's control such as depression, another mental illness, or some form of cognitive impairment. Calling suicide a death produced by a willful act of the self implies consciousness and choice, yet suicide is usually seen as an irrational behavior by a clouded mind. The *Oxford English Dictionary* (OED) defines suicide as "the act of taking one's own life," however one can also do that by accident. I will discuss some of these definitional issues in this chapter, and will hold to what I call a sufficient definition with a libertarian leaning: the act of willfully taking one's own life. This is similar to Shneidman's (1993, p. 4) definition, which he indicates applied only to the Western world: "Suicide is a conscious act of self-induced annihilation, best understood as a multidimensional malaise in a needful individual who defines an issue for which the suicide is perceived as the best solution."

Suicide Over Time

Looking at suicide has increasingly occupied the work of historians. Writers on the subject have long noted changes over time, often dramatic ones, in public attitudes toward suicide. Is suicide done consciously and deliberately? Münster and Broz (2015) refer to the tension of agency in suicide, the dialectic of agency and patiency, free will and determinism. The "passions," for example, have historically been those of acting out versus passively receiving, and Graeber (2004) points out that medieval and early modern writers had passions causing impressions on the pneumatic system and thus conditions like melancholia. Graeber shows them as logically polarized, as "either you act on the world, or the world acts on you" (p. 10). I will show that suicide has moved from a conscious and deliberate act of the self to a symptom of some disorder of thought or brain, the two viewed as independent, that cause the idea and act of suicide to take place in an individual. The historical frame is thus a perspective on changing contexts and interpretations, and as I will show later, supports a cultural understanding of suicide. History is a view of culture the long way. As Geertz (1990, p. 323) wrote, "Dealing with a world elsewhere comes to much the same thing when elsewhere is long ago as when it is far away."

Suicide appears to go back as far as human history is recorded (van Hooff, 1990), yet the OED has the word only first showing up in English print in 1651: "To vindicate oneself from . . . inevitable Calamity, by Sui-cide." The word, however, first appeared in a work by Sir Thomas Browne in 1642 (Barbagli, 2015). Suicide was seen at that time as a conscious, voluntary act, one that was judged morally. Voluntary suicide was connected for centuries to the soul's immortality, based on the models of Socrates and Christ. Personal freedom and political autonomy were long associated with suicide, informing a relationship between the individual and society and between the soul and the body. The problem of suicide in

Western society, up to the early nineteenth century when medical science gained prominence, was a problem of free will (Paperno, 1997).

One of the first records of suicide comes from the Middle Kingdom in Egypt 4,000 years ago. Historians of suicide have indicated that the idea of killing oneself has been embedded most conspicuously within the moral framework of right and wrong. Oriental sacred writings both condemned and encouraged the act. The ceremonial sacrifice of widows or suttee was institutionalized in Brahmanism in India, and in Japan suicide became a national tradition through rituals of *seppuku* and *hara-kiri*. Suicide was condemned in Judaism and the Old Testament, and Jewish custom did not allow funeral orations for suicides; while family survivors were honored, the suicides were not. In the past, suicide among Jews was rare (Farberow, 1975). In the Greek and Roman periods attitudes toward suicide were class-based, with condemnation among the lower classes but tolerance and acceptance among the higher classes. Suicide was an intentional act. With Christianity came an acceptance of martyrdom, which became common especially among women (Salisbury, 1997; Smith, 1997). Pierson (1988) describes a common "martyrdom" among slaves in seventeenth-century New England, especially those who were particularly attached to their native religions, in the belief that they would be returning to their homeland. He described "a common Afro-American conviction that drowning could be a supernatural method for returning to Africa—as well as affording an escape from slavery" (75). African slaves in Cuba killed themselves in very large numbers. As many as 20% of Africans killed themselves within their first year on the island. Chinese workers, most slaves, also killed themselves in Cuba. A great many died; they were overworked and malnourished, subjected to much cruelty, and most of the deaths were by suicide. Many killed themselves in groups, like six to eight workers found hanging from a tree (Perez, 2005).

Suicide under certain conditions in early Rome was acceptable: among women to preserve their chastity and among martyrs and ascetics. Martyrs often volunteered for public execution in early Christian Rome; their execution was also a form of mass entertainment (Salisbury, 1997). Suicide was otherwise understood as an individual's strategic solution to existential problems. Plato had suggested that sometimes suicide was rational and justifiable. The acceptability of suicide has also varied over time. Alvarez (1971) notes that in the Middle Ages, suicide was a mortal horror and depicted as such by Dante in the *Inferno*; it was made more morally complex and sophisticated during the birth of individualism— often mixed with genius and melancholy—in the Renaissance period; depicted with less imagination as somber, occasionally practical, and often mad in the Age of Reason; and in the Romantic Period, seen as agony and a way of life, "a literary act, a hysterical gesture of solidarity with whichever imaginative hero was, at that moment, the rage" (232).

Suicide was both condemned and praised in the literary genre over time (Minois, 1999), seen as tragedy, comedy, romance, satire, and deadpan (Laird, 2011).

Fear and moral revulsion were also apparent in the attitudes toward suicide in some non-Western societies. Colt (1991) describes Christian missionaries writing about their attempts to convert the Baganda people of Uganda in the mid-nineteenth century, who would burn the body of a suicide far from their community using as fuel wood from the tree or hut from which the person was found hanging. The Baganda believed that the ghost of the deceased suicide would return to impregnate young women of the tribe. The Bannuas of Cambodia buried suicides in the forest, Dahomey tribespeople left bodies of suicides to be eaten by wild animals, Native Americans of what is now Alabama threw bodies of suicides into a river while Omaha natives believed that suicides were kept from the spirit world. Iroquois and Hidatsa suicides stayed in a separate village after death, away from other souls who would be made uncomfortable. Dakota people believed suicides would always be dragging the hanging tree behind them, and apparently Dakota women hanged themselves on small trees which they would be able to more easily drag after death. The Paharis of India believed their suicides remained forever between the earth and heaven. The Wajagga of West Africa sacrificed a goat to save a suicide's soul. There is a similarity in some of these cases to Christians not burying a suicide, and as late as 1823 a suicide was buried at a London crossroads. These suicides were bad deaths, with rituals directed to ameliorate the soul and warn the living of negative sanctions to keep them from committing these acts (Colt, 1991).

Sometimes suicides went to a good place after death. Chukchee of Siberia, along with Iglulingmiut and other Inuit, believed that violent death including self-inflicted death took the person to a good place. Yet Weyer (1932, p. 251) reported that Inuit of Cumberland Sound in south Baffin, where Boas conducted his first fieldwork, believed that suicides entered a dark place called "Kumetoon" and that their tongues would loll. Ancient Celt suicides were celebrated, and Vikings of pre-Christian Scandinavia who killed themselves entered Valhalla, a place of such reverence that soldiers not dying in battle would often kill themselves with their sword to reach Valhalla. *Seppuku*, mentioned above, began in Japan 1,000 years ago and ensured the samurai a proper burial and respected memory (Colt, 1991). Within such beliefs of suicide as a good death, assisted suicide has also been performed. Inuit in the Arctic once practiced this (Balikci, 1970). Some of this attitude is seen in Western society today. Bruno Bettleheim, a former professor of mine at UCLA, killed himself believing, according to Minois (1999, p. 2), that it was a "supreme proof of liberty." Yet I learned that he was also depressed because of his wife's recent death, his own failing health and placement in a nursing home, and a major conflict with his son.

The Church officially disapproved of suicide in the fourth century ADE and legislated against it two centuries later; suicides remained low in Europe because of this through the thirteenth century. One's life belonged to God, and the taking of it was a sin. In 1284 suicides were denied a Christian burial. In France, bodies of suicides were dragged in the streets and hanged in the gallows. Alvarez (1971, p. 70) wrote that in the early Middle Ages the negative attitude toward suicide as a sin and a crime "spread like a fog across Europe because its strength came from primitive fears, prejudices and superstitions which had survived despite Christianity, Judaism and Hellenism." Seeing suicide as a type of murder made it a crime. For centuries suicide was a crime against the law and against God. Church and state worked together.

Suicide was first made illegal in England in 673 ADE, with denial of burial followed later by burial at a crossroads with a stake through the body, to the forfeiting of the suicide's property (Szasz, 1999). Trials for suicides decreased during the late eighteenth century, when government action changed with public opinion moving toward seeing suicides "more as courageous victims than as criminals" (Minois, 1999, p. 292). Colt (1991) indicates that suicide was first explained as a disease rather than a sin or a crime in 1763, in a book by a French physician named Merian. The medicalization of suicide indeed saw people killing themselves as victims, and the laws against suicide and suicide attempts changed accordingly. The Suicide Act was passed in England in 1961, under pressure from physicians, the clergy, and lawyers, making attempted suicide no longer a crime.

Suicide has also been seen as an involuntary act, at least one outside of normal, rational conscious thought. The medicalization of suicide has promoted this view, which is prevalent today. The first reference to suicide due to insanity was during Charlemagne's rule from 768–814 ADE. Robert Burton's (2001 [1621], p. 432) *Anatomy of Melancholy* pleads for mercy, in a religious context, for despairing, suicidal people, referring to them as having an "afflicted mind" and a "wounded soul." John Donne's (1982 [1647]) *Biathanatos*, written in 1608 and published after the author's death, also refers to suicide as an affliction. Donne asks for sympathy for the suicidal, admitting in the book his own inclinations toward suicide.

Kushner (1989) shows how suicide moved from being seen as a crime to a disease during the eighteenth century. Some of this transition took place within the Church. An increase was seen in England and America for suicides in court to be attributed to *non compos mentis* (uncontrolled mental state) or insanity, rather than *felo de se*, allowing the deceased to be buried in sacred ground and the death to not be listed as a suicide. MacDonald (1989) shows how *non compos mentis* verdicts on suicides rose from 8.4% in the 1660s to over 90% in the late 1700s. He indicates that it was not the medical profession that pushed the medicalization of suicide at that time but lay people, as part of the political, religious, social, and cultural environment. Kushner notes that by the end of the 1700s, religion was being seen not as a defense but more as a cause of suicide. Yet in 1725 in France a suicide was judged as murdering oneself, and the body was tied to a cart and dragged face down over the streets to a square where it was hanged upside-down from a gallow (Barbagli, 2015). There were episodes of mass suicide in Russia in the late seventeenth century, and suicides increased significantly in Europe from 1720 to 1735 (Barbagli, 2015). Barbagli (2015) notes that cognitive schemas about suicide were changing, from suicide being forbidden to becoming more tolerated. This changed significantly in the seventeenth century where acquittals became common by the end of that century, and suicides were judged to be mentally deranged rather than guilty of a crime. By the 1820s, mental illness, specifically melancholy and to a lesser degree insanity, was being associated with suicide. Physicians began subscribing to this by 1850 (MacDonald, 1989). This was related to the development of psychiatry and moral treatment, with physical/biological attributions and interventions. Suicide was referred to as a disease in an article on suicide prevention in the second year of publication of *The American Journal of Insanity* in 1845 (Article IV, 1845). Suicides were "cases of insanity," which was defined then as "a chronic disease of the brain, producing either derangement of the intellectual faculties, or prolonged change of feelings, affections, and habits of an individual" (Article I, 1844).

The relegation of suicide from crime to insanity in the nineteenth century was no guarantee of humane treatment, given the status of asylums during that time. Public county asylums were on the rise in the 1800s in Europe and the U.S., where patients/inmates were being transferred from prisons and workhouses for the poor (Jones, 1991; Shorter, 1997). Asylums were essentially warehouses until the 1930s. Suicide, like other forms of insanity, needed to be controlled and suicidal people kept out of mainstream society.

Yet in 1838 Esquirol argued that suicide was not insanity per se but a symptom, a view congruent with today's psychiatric opinion. Yet this is beginning to change with the *Diagnostic and Statistical Manual for Mental Disorders* (DSM-5; APA, 2013) where suicidality is identified as a potential mental disorder for later editions of DSM. Others, such as moral statisticians like Brierre de Boismont in 1842, would not attribute all suicides to insanity and included such causes as alcoholism, painful or incurable disease, domestic problems, sorrow and disappointment, romantic problems, poverty, ennui, and unemployment. Like Durheim half a century later, de Boismont showed that males, the unmarried, and the elderly were at higher risk for suicide. These data were supported by statistical studies in Europe and Britain. Suicide was now a medicalized problem and viewed as a symptom, and not as a rational decision by a normal individual. Yet the tension of agency was still prominent, as intention was part of the definition of suicide.

Variations in suicide were becoming known through scientific study. Morselli's (1882) statistical work found suicides in Europe to be more prevalent in the center of that continent between the latitudes of 47–57°, during the first ten days of any given month, among Protestants, in "civilized" countries, in urban rather than rural areas, and among soldiers and prisoners. Morselli also found that the method of suicide varied geographically, with common methods being drowning in Italy (where hanging was rare), hanging in Russia (where drowning was rare), firearms in southern Europe and Turkey, poisoning in Sweden, England, and Ireland (rare in France and the German states), cutting in Ireland, firearms in some large cities (e.g., New York, Geneva, Rome), and stabbing in others (e.g., London, Milan). He noted variation in method within countries, but common patterns tended to be localized. Hanging was the method of choice in the former Czechoslovakia, whereas jumping from heights has been more common in China. Suicides are done more recently by burning charcoal in France, Korea, Hong Kong, and Taiwan (Huh, Jo, Kim, Ahn, & Lee, 2009; Liu et al., 2007). Suicide is clearly based on social logic.

Morselli was in the era of moral statistics, seeing suicide as a social phenomenon. Durkheim's *Le Suicide* was the culmination of that era (Lukes, 1973). In China the most common method is the ingestion of agricultural chemicals or rat poison (Li, Xiao, & Xiao, 2009), pesticides in El Salvador and Nicaragua. In the U.S., guns are the most common method, while hanging is the most common method in Canada, Chile, South Africa, Cuba, Panama, Puerto Rico, Venezuela, Japan, and Australia (Stack, 2015). Subway suicides became very common in the 1980s as people were copying each other (Sonneck, Etzersdorfer, & Nagel-Kuess, 1994). Morselli's attributions for some of these differences within Europe fit with the psychologizing of the time toward character and behavior, with passions, love, and misery dominating the south, shame and fear of punishment the center, and alcoholism in the north of Europe. Men killed themselves more often than women because "[t]he difficulties of existence, those at least which proceed from the struggle for life, bear more heavily on man" whereas the woman "has a more impressionable nervous temperament, yet possesses the faculty of resigning herself more easily to circumstances. Self-sacrifice is, above all, the feminine virtue, as ambition is the characteristic of men" (Morselli, 1882, pp. 195, 197). Durkheim would later agree with this interpretation of sex differences in suicide.

Psychiatry was at least exposed to the sociological discourse of the nineteenth century. Motto (1993, p. 28) showed that, in 1845, the conclusion of an epidemiological report warned that the popular press should pay heed to their potential effect on suggesting suicide to readers:

> No fact . . . is better established in science, than that suicide is often committed from imitation. A single paragraph may suggest suicide to twenty persons. Some particulars of the act, or expressions, seize the imagination, and the disposition to repeat it, in a moment of morbid excitement, proves irresistible.

That same year, in the *American Journal of Insanity*, Napoleon Bonaparte's famous 1801 warning to soldiers to not kill themselves was reprinted (Miscellany, 1845). Two soldiers had killed themselves within a month. Napoleon was intent to "putting a stop at once to the spread of what appeared to be a contagious malady" (p. 93). He commanded his soldiers to not abandon life in the same way they should not abandon the battlefield. His directive may have worked, as there were no further suicides among his men for some time.

War has an interesting effect on suicide rates. They dropped significantly during the first and second world wars. Yet during the time of Nazi Germany, many Jews killed themselves. Much of this had to do with the deportations to concentration and death camps. The suicide rate among Jews during 1941–1942 was 200 per 100,000, and in Berlin this rate was 400 per 100,000 (Barbagli, 2015). Suicides among women went up. It is not known how many suicides took place in the concentration camps.

An exception to the usual historical survey of suicide is Irina Paperno's (1997) theoretical view of suicide as a cultural institution. Focusing on Russia's collective moral reality, Paperno examined the suicide epidemic in Russia between the 1860s and 1880s. The epidemic was wrapped in public consciousness as representing the moral deterioration of their society conjoined with the intellectual revolution bringing in the new medical and social sciences. Suicide was understood within "a coherent symbolic vocabulary" of the media and literature, including "'restructuring' (*perestroika*) ("in a pessimistic vein"), 'decomposition . . . of the life order', 'a time of difficult transition' . . . or 'a transition between the old and the new'" (p. 46). Stories of suicide became commonplace in the newspapers, with lines like "Among young people suicide mania has definitely become a social disease, taking on greater dimensions every day" (p. 76). And journalists wrote of metaphoric realities, of suicide's "root cause" being in the social "soil" (p. 87). In her book, Paperno demonstrates that suicide is embedded in culture, in the case of this Russian epidemic through media, literature, legal debates, and reforms, as part of a more general coherent collective thinking and behavior. It can be cognitive sociology, where thinking is very socially influenced (Zerubavel, 1997).

By the 1960s, suicide was viewed by most scholars and clinicians working in the area as a "multidimensional malaise" (Shneidman, 1985,

p. 203). Many of these dimensions seem incongruous with each other: suicide as a symptom of mental illness or severe distress; as aggression turned toward the self; as abnormal serotonin levels in the brain; as escape from unbearably painful consciousness; as the weight of unbearable social forces; as a cluster of personality/cognitive traits; as problem-solving deficits. Much of the incongruity stems from the absence of theory in suicide studies tying the various dimensions together, with many smaller-level theories centered on the various dimensions and often implicitly but sometimes explicitly dismissing the alternatives. The historical frame has provided the perspective of there having been multiple perspectives, which continues. There has been a gradual move over time from seeing suicide as voluntary to involuntary. When the individual is believed to have made a personal decision about suicide, it has been, from most perspectives, viewed as bad. As a symptom of mental illness or other despair, suicide has still been viewed as morally bad but also as mad and irrational, justifying control over a person's liberty while he or she is in such a state. The individual is not held personally responsible for a decision that has been caused by mental illness or such acute distress that one's rational mind is no longer fully available (see Horwitz, 2002). Edwin Shneidman (1987), the dean of suicidology, wrote that one should never make such an important decision as suicide while suicidal, i.e., psychologically distressed. When this decision has been based on social ritual or expectation, on group consensus, the view has ranged from tolerable to celebrated. Rather than being historicist, most histories of suicide have been chronological with the identification of the common thoughts about and practices toward the idea of suicide over time. These histories highlight the complexity and poor understanding of suicide over a great deal of time. We will now look at the various frames that suicide has been placed in.

Biological Suicide

Considerations of an organic component or basis for suicide go back at least a few centuries, but specific research on this did not begin until the 1940s. In 1733 George Cheyne published *The English Malady* and suggested that the English had a "nervous distemper" making them more prone to suicide because of their rich foods, lack of exercise, and city pollution. In his 1758 *A Treatise on Madness*, William Battle mentioned hot, cold, and damp weather as being related to suicide (Colt, 1991). It is interesting that Kushner (1989) suggested that the high protein diets of Germans, Austrians, and Danes would lower their serotonin levels, and thus likely contribute to their relatively higher suicide rates.

Shorter (1997) describes two eras of biological psychiatry. The first occurred in the 1800s when a clinical-pathological model was being applied in medical research. This followed from the New Science of the seventeenth century and the Enlightenment. Porter (1996a) referred to the nineteenth century as revolutionary for medical science, and as the age of the rise and fall of the asylum (Porter, 1996b). Much biological research in psychiatry took place in Germany and Austria during this time, with a focus on tissues, nerves, brains, chemistry, and the use of the microscope. Again, in the 1870s Charcot named "hysteria" and thought it to be organic and genetically transmitted. It was after the influence of Kraepelin, Meyer, and Freud that the second biological psychiatry began, according to Shorter, in the 1970s with the displacing of psychoanalysis as the major paradigm in psychiatry. This was in spite of physical etiologies being considered and treatments being used before then. Genetics became a prevalent model with twin and adoption studies (see Segal, 1999). Psychopharmacology also gained a foothold in psychiatry, beginning in the 1920s but flourishing after the 1950s and '60s. Biological psychiatry is stronger now than it has ever been, from current television commercials for psych meds to this time being called the Age of Prozac.

Motto (1992) found the first modern biological-etiological reference to suicide in 1954, with a high versus low urinary norepinephrine/epinephrine ratio hypothesized to be related to the Freudian turning of anger out versus in, respectively. A 1965 study by Bunney and Fawcett found elevated 17-hydroxycorticosteroid levels in patients who killed themselves, although later studies of noradrenergic activity and suicide have not supported a relationship. Since the 1980s, studies have linked low 5-hydroxyindoleacetic acid (5-HIAA), the serotonin metabolite, with suicide and more violent suicide attempts (see earlier study by Åsberg, Träskman, & Thoren, 1976). It is not clear whether low 5-HIAA levels are state or trait, premorbidly, or whether serotonin responds to particular mood states shortly before suicide. Or maybe serotonin just stays stable before a suicide.

Marcia Angell (2011a, 2011b) reviewed recent books on psychopharmacology and psychiatry for the *New York Review of Books*. She highlighted that there is no evidence for any chemical imbalance being related to a mental disorder or symptom. The theory that low serotonin was the cause of depression came from antidepressants raising serotonin in the brain. Backwards reasoning, Angell suggests, a great leap in logic. As she put it, it is like thinking that fevers are caused by too little aspirin. There is similarly little to no evidence for a neurobiological cause of suicide (Whitaker, 2010). Yet the research continues.

Serum cortisol levels were found elevated for suicides by Krieger (1974), but this has not been replicated (Meltzer & Lowy, 1989). The metabolites of dopamine (homovanillic acid) and norepinephrine (3-methoxy-4-hydroxyphenolglycol), dysregulation of the hypothalamic-pituitary-thyroid axis, corticotrophin releasing factor (CRF) levels, cerebrospinal fluid magnesium, and genes have also been studied for suicide, with mixed and inconclusive results (Motto, 1992). Studies of the neurotransmitters serotonin, dopamine, and norepinephrine have been associated with mood disorders; however teasing suicide from particular types of disturbed mood in research remains the most significant challenge.

There has been research on genetics and suicide (Bondy, Buettner, & Zill, 2006). Tryptophan hydroxylase and TPH1 genes have been studied, and both have received mixed results with many negative findings. The genetic contribution to suicide is weaker than the environmental one (Brezo, Klempan, & Turecki, 2008). Molecular genetics studies are inconclusive. Twin studies, however, are suggestive, with higher concordance rates for monozygotic versus dizygotic twins. For completed suicides, they were 6.93 times greater for biological versus adoptive relatives (Baldessarini & Hennen, 2004). There is thus strong support for familial risk of suicide (Brent & Melhem, 2008; Roy, Rylander, & Sarchiapone, 1977). This may be environmental and imitative.

Advances in the biology of suicide continue, and psychologist/suicidologist David Jobes (2003) announced that the "first frontier" of mental illness and suicide is the study of neuroscience, neurobiology, and genetics. Kay Redfield Jamison, another psychologist, promotes antidepressant medication as suicide prevention around the world in her lectures. She makes the argument for a strong genetic predisposition for suicide, and in her popular book on suicide argues that the social variations found for suicide, from seasons to nations, likely parallel the same variations for mental disorders such as schizophrenia, depression, and mania (Jamison, 1999). Unfortunately, although Jamison's bibliography is rich, the erroneous absence of any research citations in the text makes it difficult to look for the relevant research reports to confirm this assertion.

We are still Cartesian, separating mind from body and, in health-related fields, both from culture. How could neurochemistry not both respond to and affect, or share identity with, thoughts-emotions? There is strong support for individual differences in temperament, likely continuous from birth, which also likely contributes to vulnerability to more extreme mood states and behaviors (Kagan, 1998). Yet as humans we are remarkably adaptive, and any deterministic model of human behavior, whether biological, psychological, or cultural, will be severely limited by this fact (Lewis, 1997). I later propose a middle-level theory of suicide focusing strongly on culture, however I agree with Kagan (1998) that multiple sources of evidence are needed for a deeper understanding of any human phenomenon.

Psychological Frames

The psychological and psychiatric frameworks, which I combine here because of their focus on the individual, dominate the literature in suicide studies or suicidology. A book entitled *Essential Papers on Suicide* (Maltsberger & Goldblatt, 1996), one of a series by NYU Press, contains 40 reprinted papers, and all but two, one on biology and the other on sociology, neither of which are representative of those disciplines' works on suicide, are on psychology or psychiatry. Psychological/psychiatric topics are also the norm at the annual conferences of the Canadian Association for Suicide Prevention and the American Association of Suicidology, and this has been the case across the histories of the two associations. Psychological approaches to suicidal behavior have examined a wide range of topics. I will summarize below the seven primary theoretical angles addressed by this literature.

Suicide as Escape

"There is, I believe, a whole class of suicides . . . who take their own lives not in order to die but to escape confusion, to clear their heads," wrote Alvarez (1971). Friedrich Engels wrote in 1845 that suicide was a form of escape (Barbagli, 2015). Psychological theories have as one core motivational theme the escape from unbearable consciousness. By 1910 Freud had linked escape from humiliation with suicide (Litman, 1967, and later Menninger (1938) highlighted escape as one of the motives behind the act. Shneidman (1985) has identified egression as one of the commonalities across all suicides, and Baumeister (1990) and Maris (1992) have focused on escape within their theoretical models of suicide. Baumeister's theory is the most comprehensive, viewing suicide as escape from a despised self. He had six steps that lead to suicide: having unrealistically high expectations (perfectionism) and recent problems or setbacks or having a high contrast between high expectations and poor outcomes, blaming oneself, negative emotion, a deconstructed mental state such as low levels of awareness, avoidance of decisions and responsibility, and the reduction of inhibitions. The person is preoccupied with him- or herself. Baumeister cited evidence such as suicide being higher in U.S. states that have a better quality of life, suicide being higher in societies that endorse individual freedom, and suicide being higher with downward social mobility. For Baumeister, the escape is from a very aversive self. Dean, Range, and Goggin (1996) found that when college students think that others have unrealistically high expectations of them, they are more suicidal. Dean and Range (1999) found support for Baumeister's theory with clinical outpatients, finding that socially prescribed perfectionism led to depression, hopelessness, and suicidal ideation. It was found that for suicidal adolescents, escape was the primary motive for the attempt, to obtain relief from stress and psychological pain (Boergers, Spirito, & Donaldson, 1998). Others have argued that some individuals with enduring psychological defensive styles of escape, who are faced with an unambiguously confronted negative self, under threat or condition of public exposure, may logically select suicide as another yet extreme form of escape (Kral & Johnson, 1996). Shneidman (1993) saw suicide as escape from severe psychological pain or what he termed psychache. Szasz (1999, p. 58) has summarized this suicidal scenario as a person who "feels trapped, often because he has suffered a grave defeat." Psychologically, suicide has been viewed as the avoidance of suffering rather than a longing to be dead.

Suicide as Hopelessness and Helplessness

Hopelessness and helplessness have long been themes in studies of suicide (Farberow & Shneidman, 1961; Shneidman, Farberow, & Litman, 1970). It has been found that clinicians' ratings of a patient's level of hopelessness, or the same rated by the patient on Beck's Hopelessness Scale (Beck, Weissman, Lester, & Trexler, 1974), is one of the best longitudinal predictors of eventual suicide among suicidal patients presenting to a clinic (Beck, Steer, Kovacs, & Garrison, 1985; Beck, Brown, & Steer, 1989; Weishaar & Beck, 1992). Suicide is interpreted as giving up, of seeing no positive future and no relief from suffering. Minkoff, Bergman, Beck, and Beck (2006) found that negative expectations was a strong indicator of suicidal intent, and Wetzel, Margulies, Davis, and Karam (1980) found hopelessness related to suicidal intent. Yet Cole (1989) did not find hopelessness to be related to suicidality among a group of adolescents. Hopelessness depression has been identified as a subtype of the disorder, characterized by the attribution of one's negative life events to stable and global causes; it involves a particular vulnerability to suicidal ideation and behavior (Abramson, Metalsky, & Alloy, 1989). Van Orden, Cukrowicz, Braithwaite, Selby, and Joiner (2010) suggested that hopelessness related to thwarted belongingness and perceived burdensomeness is why suicidal ideation and behavior occurs. This is discussed further below. Flipping to its positive side, a focus on hope has become one of the key topics in the new "positive" psychology and the study of well-being and mental health (Carver & Scheier, 2002; Gillham, 2000; Vaillant, 2003).

Suicide as Irrationality

Suicide as disturbed thinking is also much in the literature, particularly the focus on illogical thinking (Neuringer & Lettieri, 1971; Shneidman & Farberow, 1970). Within the popular theory of depression as distorted thinking (Beck, 1967, 1987), suicide has been studied as the result of cognitive or problem-solving deficits such as rigidity, dichotomous thinking, and "tunnel vision" or the inability to consider alternatives (Adams & Adams, 1996; Schotte & Clum, 1987). Some have indicated that poor problem-solving is associated with being suicidal (Ellis & Rutherford, 2008). Dour, Cha, and Nock (2011) found that poor problem-solvers with emotional reactivity were associated with suicide attempts. Irrational beliefs, impaired decision making, poor problem-solving, deductive fallacies, dichotomous thinking, cognitive rigidity, cognitive constriction, and cognitive distortions are association with suicidality (Ellis & Ratliff, 1986; Jager-Hyman et al., 2014; Jollant et al., 2005; Neuringer, 1961, 1964; Reinecke, 2006; Shneidman, 1985; Wilson, Stelzer, Bergman, & Kral, 1995). Cognitive-behavioral therapies have been directed for suicidal people, with some success (Ellis & Newman, 1996; Freeman, Reineke, & Beck, 1993; Lerner & Clum, 1990; Linehan, Armstrong, Suarez, Allmon, & Heard, 1991). Suicidal people are thus cognitively different from nonsuicidal people (Ellis, 2006a).

Suicide as Symptom

Suicide is seen as a symptom of mental illness (Joiner, Hom, Hagan, & Silva, 2016), where the term "symptom" is used as a heuristic medical metaphor. In psychology and psychiatry, suicidality is typically described as a real symptom of mental illness, e.g., of depression alongside other symptoms in psychiatry's *Diagnostic and Statistical Manual for Mental Disorders* (DSM) such as insomnia, fatigue, and weight loss (APA, 2013). It is something that "naturally" happens and is inevitable when one crosses one's threshold of tolerance for subjective distress (Menninger, 1938; Motto, 1992). Suicide is a symptom thus caused by suffering.

Suicide is co-morbid with other "symptoms," particularly impulsivity/aggression, depression, hopelessness, anxiety, and self-consciousness/social disengagement (Conner, Duberstein, Conwell, Seidlitz, & Caine, 2001). Research has identified short-term (one year or less) psychological risk factors for completed suicide among Americans. Among depressed patients, the co-occurrence of severe anxiety or agitation, e.g., worry, fear, and panic attacks, becomes a significant short-term predictor of suicide. Further argument for suicide as a symptom comes from studies, largely post-mortem and thus retrospective, indicating that approximately 90% suicides have had a diagnosable mental disorder (Bertolote & Fleischmann, 2002). The most common disorder in these studies is depression (Blair-West, Cantor, Mellsop, & Eyeson-Annan, 1999). Suicide thus becomes a reified medical symptom rather than a metaphor, and the cause is largely psychic and sometimes physical "pain" that, in most cases, is associated with a mental disorder. As a symptom, suicide also becomes directly tied to mental disorders and thus assumed to be causally linked to neurochemical or even DNA disregulation. And as a symptom, there is a deterministic side to suicide—a medical symptom caused by an illness.

Suicide as Unconscious Motivation

Although he published only a few pages on suicide, Freud's notion of suicide as outward aggression or anger turned toward the self became a popular staple regarding the psychology of self-destruction. This was first proposed by Wilhelm Stekel at a meeting in Freud's apartment in 1910 as a self-directed murderous wish outside of conscious awareness (Shneidman, 1969). The suicidal person has identified with someone he or she loves and hates, and the ambivalent feelings are turned inward in unconscious sadism. Strong aggressive impulses failed to express outwardly and are turned inward (Jackson, 1957). This more general idea was already well known; for example in German the term for suicide has long been *selbsmord*, or self-murder. For Freud (1917), suicide made little psychological sense unless, he posited, the self or ego was split such that one kills a separate part of the self that has been identified with a loved and now lost or bad other. According to Eyman and Kulick (1996, p. 39), for Freud "the very act of suicide always involved the unconscious fantasy of not the self being killed but this ambivalently regarded person or ideal being destroyed." Aggression and its management were essential to both suicide and to human functioning in general in his theorizing. Later, Karl Menninger (1933) argued that suicide was motivated by three necessary and sufficient unconscious motivations: the wish to kill, the wish to be killed, and the wish to die. The wish to kill was the wish to destroy the psychological representation of this other person, the wish to be killed came from unconscious guilt and suicide becomes a death penalty, and the wish to die is driven by the death instinct that Freud thought everybody had (Eyman & Kulick, 1996). Carl Jung's analytic psychology has also influenced thinking about suicide. The Jungian analyst Hillman (1964) wrote that suicide must be understood within the context of a person's inner mythology, in which he included dreams and fantasies. He called it "the most alarming problem of life" (p. 16). For Jung, suicide was an attempt at transformation (Lester, 1996a). Hendin (1991) wrote that the psychodynamics of suicide see it as a response to loss, separation, or abandonment. There may be feelings of rage from the experience of a loss, and self-punishment may be related to feeling responsible for the loss. The rage may be toward lost love. Suicide is an attempt at transformation and rebirth (Lester, 1996a), and motivated by self-protection rather than self-destruction (Kral & Johnson, 1996). A psychodynamic approach to suicide examines emotional and cognitive states, close relationships and object loss, both conscious and unconscious meanings given to death, and defense mechanisms congruent with self-annihilation (Hendin, 1991; Maltsberger, 1999).

Suicide as Psychache or Unbearable Psychological Pain

This is the theory of Edwin Shneidman, who coined the term suicidology and founded the American Association of Suicidology. Shneidman felt that a person's needs were not being met, especially what he called vital needs, those most important to the person. These needs are frustrated and cause what he called psychache, which causes suicide. He wrote that,

> For the suicidal person, that psychological pain, that pain in the mind, that psychache, has a quantitative intensity that pushes it into a special qualitative state; it is deemed unbearable, intolerable, unacceptable; it has crossed a certain critical line somewhere in the mind.
> (Shneidman, 1998, p. 248)

Psychache can be any type of psychological pain. Shneidman (1993, p. 147) has written that "suicide is caused by psychache" and describes his neologism as being

> intrinsically psychological—the pain of excessively felt shame, or guilt, or humiliation, or loneliness, or fear, or angst, or dread of growing old or of dying badly, or whatever. . . . Suicide occurs when the psychache is deemed by that person to be unbearable.

Holden, Mehta, Cunningham, and Lindsay (2001) created a psychache scale, and Patterson and Holden (2012) found that psychache was a better predictor of suicidal ideation than depression, hopelessness, and lack of meaning in life. Campos, Gomes, Holden, Piteira, and Rainha (2017) found that psychache mediated the relationship between suicidal ideation and frequency of psychological symptoms in a sample of community adults. Shneidman (1971) had an earlier theory that suicide is caused by perturbation and lethality. Perturbation is any kind of upset, while lethality was the probability that the act will have a lethal outcome, how deathfully suicidal or oriented toward death a person is. Elsewhere he had lethality as the deadliness of the suicide method. Yet in his book on suicide as psychache (Shneidman, 1995), he wrote that perturbation and lethality are both necessary for suicide. He wrote, "No one has ever died from elevated perturbation alone. It is elevated lethality that is dangerous to life" (p. 7). That is this book's premise, with a different definition of lethality. But then Shneidman goes on to write that psychache or perturbation causes suicide without mentioning lethality. This seems to be a contradiction. Yet in his last book, Shneidman (2008, p. 139) wrote, "The basic formula for suicide is rather straightforward: introspective torture plus the idea of death as release." This is the premise of my book. Shneidman did not include "the idea of death as release" in his theory.

The Interpersonal Theory of Suicide

This is a theory produced by Thomas Joiner (2005). His is a three-component theory of suicide, seeing suicide as caused by perceived failed belongingness, which is similar to Durheim's lack of integration in society, perceived burdensomeness, and accrued lethality. The first two components are the interpersonal ones. Baumeister and Leary (1995) suggest that the need to belong is a fundamental human need. Van Orden, Witte, Gordon, Bender, and Joiner (2008) found that both thwarted belongingness and high perceptions of burdensomeness are needed for suicidal ideation, rather than just thwarted belongingness. Yet both can cause passive suicidal ideation. Thwarted belongingness can result in self-defeating behavior, including suicidal behavior. Perceived burdensomeness has two dimensions of interpersonal functioning: belief that the self is so flawed as to be a liability on others and emotionally laden thoughts of self-hatred, which includes low self-esteem, self-blame, and shame, as well as being mentally agitated (Van Orden et al., 2010). Two fundamental needs are not met: the need to belong and the need to feel effective (the opposite of being a burden). When these needs are thwarted, this leads to a desire for death. Joiner sees most suicides as planned. Social isolation is a predictor of suicidal ideation. The theory used the principle of opponent-process, where when the effects of a provocative stimulus diminish, its opposite effect is strengthened. He indicates this is a bit is like skydiving, which becomes easier with practice. Suicide follows this same process. Accrued lethality is a learned habit; it is when one gets used to pain or seeing harmful events. One does not fear death anymore. Joiner reports, for example, that suicidal people have higher pain thresholds. This acquired capability for suicide is learned. It includes increased physical pain tolerance and reduced fear of death through habituation, including repeated exposure to physically painful or fear-inducing experiences. There is repeated practice and exposure, so the person gets used to it. A recent criticism of this theory shows it to be intrapersonal, decontextualized, reductionist, and problematic in that it explains all suicides everywhere (Hjelmeland & Knizek, 2019).

Vulnerability

A psychological frame worthy of exploration is that of what I have called "receptive shores," the openness or vulnerability, depending on one's stance concerning suicide, to the idea of self-destruction applied to oneself (Kral, 1998). It is here where culture and psychology meet, where a social ideology or cultural model comes to rest in an individual mind, referred to as the process of internalization. Edward Sapir (1934, p. 414) called this "an important fact, systematically ignored by the cultural anthropologist," when "we see at once elements of culture that come well within the horizon of awareness of one individual entirely absent in another individual's landscape." This is also known as the stress-diathesis model of mental disorders and suicide, where there is a combination of vulnerable people plus external stress (Heeringen, 2012).

The concept of psychological vulnerability offers a significant clue on the individual side of this equation. Alcohol and drug abuse is one factor, and psychiatric disorders, most notably depression, are strongly indicated. Shneidman's concept of perturbation or psychache is, arguably, the underlying psychological experience behind all demographic and experiential correlates of suicide. Psychological pain leaves one vulnerable, and the current view of Shneidman (1993) is that this pain *causes* suicide. Yet most people experiencing great psychological pain will not kill themselves. We are still left with wondering which individuals select this idiom of suicide, and why. Does it perhaps select them, or is there an interaction, a dialectic, that needs to be explored? One possibility for a dialectical understanding may involve the notion of escape. Suicide, as mentioned, has in the psychological literature been viewed as a form of escape. The motivation for suicide is understood as escape from intolerable distress or consciousness. Baumeister (1990) has argued that suicide is an escape from the self, in this case a negative self that is to be avoided at all costs. This avoidance has included the avoidance of emotions, particularly negative emotions and negative memories. Under severe duress this can include what Baumesister calls cognitive deconstruction, a restricted mode of thinking. Baumeister's model has a formulaic approach in which all people under an aggregate of certain conditions will become suicidal. I have elsewhere suggested that suicide as escape will be more likely internalized if it fits with escape tendencies of individuals (Kral & Johnson, 1996). The dynamic "connectives" would be much the same as what Baumeister described, in which the idea of suicide finds a home. Males, for example, may be more likely to use unconscious escapist mechanisms than women, and males have a much higher suicide rate than women in most of the world. Males may thus see suicide as escape as a better fit with their usual defense modes than females. Vulnerable people may choose suicide as an option. But where does this idea come from? I do not believe that psychological pain or psychache, or even escape motivation, causes suicide. All it causes is a desire to stop suffering.

Durkheim, Sociology, and the Collective Force

Durkheim's *Le Suicide* (1951, [1897]) has been the grand sociological treatise on the subject for over a century. Durkheim minimized individual factors as *causally* contributing to suicide, and instead focused on what he called the "collective force" of society (p. 299). Examining suicide statistics, i.e., rates, in great detail for various countries and social groups, he found that they manifested local stability over time yet reliably differentiated groups of people on the basis of nationality, religion, marital status, social ties, and social integration and regulation. He argued that neither details of a person's immediate situation, such as disappointment or illness, nor a person's "intrinsic nature" such as personality/temperament or psychiatric disorder, could account for these suicide rates. He found larger social conditions to be related to these rates, and characterized them as types of suicide. Durkheim was a social realist, with his familiar methodological and moral injunction that social facts are "things" (*comme des choses*), concrete entities worthy of attention by the intellectuals of his time. Social facts, "ways of acting, thinking, and feeling . . ." were "endowed with a power of coersion" and thus had motivational force on the individual (Durkheim, 1964, p. 3 [1938]). *Des choses* (things) was used persuasively to communicate in ordinary language about everyday reality. The morality behind his vocabulary concerned what he believed was a new way of thinking about society and ethics. Social characteristics related to the incidence of suicide were as real as suicide rates, as real as an individual's death.

The four types of suicide identified by Durkheim were features of collective life corresponding to ways people are more or less connected to each other. Integration and regulation were key concepts of his theory of the social bond, the first tying the individual to society and the second identifying an organizational principle of social groups. Too little or too much integration and regulation caused suicide. At the center of his theory of suicide was the integration of the person into the collective: "suicide varies inversely with the degree of integration of the original groups of which the individual forms a part" (Durkheim, 1951, p. 209 [1897]). The first type of suicide was *egoistic*, for those not sufficiently integrated into important social groups such as family or within their society. People living alone in cities fell into this group. These are people who feel they do not belong, which is now part of Joiner's theory. A second type of suicide, caused by under-regulation, was *anomic*. Anomic suicide was caused by excessive and rapid social change that disrupts the regulatory function of norms, expectations, and social life. It is the loss of a social compass. Durkheim believed that the move toward individualism taking place during his time was having a markedly negative effect on society, breaking apart families and other bonds that had held people together as a meaningful collective. Anomie was a result of social change caused by urbanization, industrialism, and secularism—modernism—in and of Western society, and suicide was one of the consequences. A third type was *altruistic*, in which, by contrast, people are excessively over-integrated and kill themselves through conformity. War-related or mass suicides would fall into this category. When people are over-regulated, *fatalistic* becomes a fourth type of suicide whereby the individual loses any sense of control over his or her participation in society. In a study of American suicide notes, Peck (1983) found that a third of them, more than would otherwise be expected in the general population, showed an external locus of control—attributions of one's life being controlled externally rather than through a sense of agency. Durkheim viewed his time as one of collective sadness as a result of this modernism (Stack, 1994), what he called the "state of crisis and perturbation" of his civilization (Durkheim, 1951 p. 369 [1897]). His ideas about egoism and anomie were rooted in discussions of his day on the causes of social disintegration (Lukes, 1973). Durkheim might have agreed that he had identified a form of social suffering that today is viewed as caused by social forces (Kleinman, Das, & Lock, 1997), even though his writing did not reflect current notions of psychic pain.

Cultural sociologists Seth Abrutyn and Anna Mueller have extended Durkheim's theory of suicide. Integration and regulation operate together (Abrutyn, 2017). Abrutyn (2017) sees Durkheim's four types of suicide as being shame-based, shame being when it is believed that other people appraise a self as deficient. Abrutyn and Mueller see regulation as cultural directives (Mueller & Abrutyn, 2016). Cultural directives are "the guidelines/rules for identifying, labeling, and expressing emotions; evaluating and understanding attitudes; and determining appropriate goals and the 'right' line of action for achieving these goals" (Abrutyn & Mueller, 2015, p. 6). A cultural directive can become a suicide script. Suicide becomes a cultural directive when it becomes a viable option to people who do not fit in or do not live up to other cultural directives. Suicide risk goes up. Cultural directives can be positive or negative based on the person's social ties. School-based suicide clusters can be seen through cultural directives. Abrutyn and Mueller (2018) show that cultural directives permitting suicide in a school influence students through personal role models, high status models, and more students adopting a cultural practice and these ideas spreading. In a recent study they found that "after repeated exposure to suicide, [a] community's cultural script for suicide may have been rekeyed such that suicide became a more imaginable option for some community youth" (Abrutyn, Mueller, & Osborne, in press).

There is a conformity taking place.

Durkheim's book on suicide is often attributed to the founding of sociology, a discipline he was seeking to regulate. His influence has been enormous, with societies, journals, books, and a plethora of academic productivity around his ideas and work. I will focus on two of his ideas in particular and link them with more current work on suicide: the notion of collective representations or mentalities, and the kinds of suicide called egoistic and anomic, respectively addressing problems of low social integration and regulation. My sense, however, is that Durkheim was wrong. His four types of suicides are not related to suicide but to perturbation, to states of upset. Lukes (1973) indicates that one criticism of Durkheim's theory is that he does not address why psychological distress should lead to suicide, why certain people are prone to suicide. He even said that the social causes resulted in a "state of crisis and perturbation," and "the causes of the general malaise currently being undergone by European societies" (Durkheim, 1951, p. 37). Why then suicide? I will show that perturbation is only one component of suicide, and it does not cause suicide. It causes vulnerability. The second component, the critical one, is ideational: the idea of suicide.

Collective Representations

When Durkheim (1951 [1897]) wrote of the collective force in *Le Suicide*, which he described as *le conscience collective* in his 1893 book *The Division of Labour*, he described collective representations as modes of thought in group form. Cognitive thought had a social origin. He was a social determinist. He was thus also an idealist, in addition to a materialist supporter of a social reality. In this work Durkheim (1951, p. 312 [1897]) argued that "essentially social life is made up of representations," noting that these representations have their own laws unlike those of individual representations, and as such should be called social psychology. His *conscience collective* was made up of collective beliefs and sentiments, according to Lukes (1973). Durkheim thus foreshadowed cognitive anthropology. It is important to note here that Durkheim's position centered on mental or cognitive representations at the group or societal/cultural level, which had much to do with group structural solidarity and social regulation. Taylor (1994) argues that he was inconsistent regarding his idealist/cognitive versus materialist/social structural views. Taylor also points out that Durkheim was inconsistent regarding his views about where the individual or psychology fit into his scheme, and shows that he retained the individual in his focus yet pointed to social factors regarding the cause of certain behaviors like suicide. Society was in the individual.

As was common in nineteenth-century social discourse, Durkheim (1951 [1897]) used body and medical metaphors to describe social reality: "collective asthenia, or social malaise" representing "the physiological distress of the body social" (p. 214). But Durkheim transferred the locus of attention from the body to the collective through the language of embodiment. Notes Paperno (1997, p. 43), for Durkheim

> an individual taken singly . . . is as good as dead, but within the collective personality, the individual receives life. In a similar fashion, the external can become the internal. Thus, what is external for the individual body is internal for the collective body. Moreover, because the individual is absorbed by the collective body, an external state actually becomes an internal state. . . . Within the collective personality, the self is the other.

Material positivism and idealism were thus brought together within the body metaphor, which contained the human mind. For Paperno, the ambiguity between the individual and the collective, the real and the metaphoric, is thus resolved. As Durkheim (1951, p. 213 [1897]) wrote, "Man is double, that is because social man superimposes himself upon physical man."

That Durkheim kept the individual within his theoretical frame is seen in the emphasis on integration with regard to suicide. It was obvious that only the individual can decide on and perform this act, so Durkheim saw societal reasons centered on the move toward individualism that would account for the social disconnect he linked to individual vulnerability. He was interested in "the ways in which social and cultural factors influence, indeed largely constitute, individuals" (Lukes, 1973, p. 13). A disconnect is also seen in his fatalistic type of suicide, where the person is disconnected from participating meaningfully in the larger social group. Lukes (1973, p. 232) indicates that while Durkheim was a socialist of his own kind, he only once and very briefly discussed any link to Marxism. Durkheim's dissertation was on the relationship between individualism and socialism, and while he focused on the latter he did not dismiss persons in spite of later accusations of this. His critique of individualism concerned primarily the breakdown of social solidarity rather than a critique of psychological aspects of suicide. Even in his "debate" with sociologist Gabriel Tarde, a methodological individualist who saw persons at the center of society, Durkheim stated that Tarde had misunderstood him as dismissing the person (Lukes, 1973, p. 303). In 1875 James Tufts criticized Durkheim using the words of John Stuart Mill: "Men are not, when brought together, converted into another kind of substance" (Lukes, 1973, p. 314). Even Malinowski accused Durkheim of downplaying the individual while at the same time using "individual psychological explanations" in his theory (Lukes, 1973, p. 523). Durkheim believed that excessive egoism is the product of social factors, based on, or modeled after, social representations. For Durkheim, social representations made up social reality: "*nous avions dit expressément et répété de touts les manières que la vie sociale était toute entière faite des representations.*" Shared representations for Durkheim are social institutions, argues Bloor (2001, p. 338), and as the "currency of interaction" they are constitutive of such interactions. Representations are socially constructed, as Durkheim wrote about religion, saying that "sacred beings exist only in and through their representations" and "there is perhaps no collective representation that is not in a sense delusive; religious beliefs are only a special case of a very general law" (Durkheim, 1995 [1912], pp. 349, 228). Durkheim noted the relationship between personal and collective representations:

> Solely because society exists, there also exists beyond sensations and images a whole system of representations that possess marvelous properties. By means of them, men understand one another, and minds gain access to one another. They have a kind of force and moral authority by virtue of which they impose themselves upon

individual minds. From then on, the individual realizes, at least dimly, that above his private representations there is a world of type-ideas according to which he has to regulate his own; he glimpses a whole intellectual world in which he participates but which is greater than he.

(p. 438)

Using more contemporary terms, Durkheim posited that culture is ideational or cognitive, that culture has motivational force and is internalized into individual minds, and that the whole is greater and certainly more complex than the sum of its parts. The individual, according to Durkheim, was embedded in a larger cognitive system. Can suicide be a social representation that motivates vulnerable people to do it?

Durkheim viewed society as static rather than dynamic, as did most anthropologists of his time, and society was ideally organized around an ideational equilibrium or equilibria. This was also the view of Kroeber and Kluckhohn (1963, p. 357 [1952]) in their classic work on culture, whose widely held definition of culture included patterns "of and for behaviour acquired and transmitted by symbols," and had an ideational focus. Unlike Durkheim, as anthropology's representatives Kroeber and Kluckhohn added the importance of the person: "*Concretely*, [culture] is created by individual organisms operating as a group. It is internalized in individuals and also becomes part of their environment through the medium of other individuals and of cultural products" (p. 367). Yet Durkheim's influence on Radcliffe-Brown and functionalism in British anthropology (e.g., the integrative functions of myth in society), and on Lévy-Strauss and structuralism in French anthropology, has been enormous (Adams, 1998). It is worth noting here that North American anthropology was early on more influenced by German sociology and the other great sociologist of that time, Max Weber (e.g., via Parsons). Durkheim worked with social statistics at some remove, while Weber contributed *verstehen* to method—the imaginative understanding or empathy of the other—and his view of humans in search of meaning (Lindholm, 2007). Weber (1949 [1904]), p. 81) resembled and perhaps borrowed from Malinowski, for example, when he wrote, "All knowledge of cultural reality, as may be seen, is always from *particular points of view*" (italics in original); Hall (1999, p. 128) cites Weber as the "classic exemplar" of hermeneutics.

The study of collective ideation, however, has been central to anthropology. The linking of such ideation to individuals has been the domain of the subdisciplines of psychological and cognitive anthropology. Ties between anthropology and psychology, disciplines with some fundamentally different epistemologies, were made by earlier anthropologists ranging from Sapir, Mead, Benedict, Rivers, and Malinowski, to Boas (see Stocking, 1992a). The view of culture as cognition in anthropology is not new, but a smaller number of anthropologists are examining how individual cognition is mediated by culture. Culture and cognition has been included in anthropology's traditional study of cultural difference, however the newer look is a critique of psychic unity—the assumption that all minds are alike save for cultural content (Shore, 1996). These subdisciplines in anthropology investigating culture and mind have employed constructs such as cultural and personal schemas or models, which are conceptual structures that are "frequent, well organized, memorable, made from minimal cues, and resistant to change" (Lindholm, 2007, p. 257). Schemas are not internalized by everyone. It is a modern version of the Durkheimian notion of collective and individual representations, but with a commitment to the study of how they are mutually constituted (e.g., Cole & Scribner, 1974; D'Andrade, 1995; Holland & Quinn, 1987; Shweder & LeVine, 1984; Shweder, 2003; Strauss & Quinn, 1997), including how culture produces human motivation (D'Andrade & Strauss, 1992; Munro et al., 1997). Psychology has likewise moved in a similar direction with cultural psychology (e.g., Bruner, 1990; Farr & Moscovici, 1984; Kirshner & Whitson, 1997; Resnick, Levine, & Teasley, 1991; Rosen, 1995), including social psychology's re-discovery of social representations (Moscovici, 1981). Such work in anthropology and psychology is still relatively marginalized within each of these disciplines, however studies at their crossroads are on the rise.

Anomie and Egoism

Although much can be said about suicide related to over-regulation (fatalism) and over-integration (altruism), more attention has been paid in the literature to low regulation (anomie) or low integration (egoism) and suicide given that these are said to be more common social factors in Western democratic societies. Egoism and anomie were a sign of society's insufficient presence in individuals (Durkheim, 1951). Indeed, as mentioned previously, Durkheim (1951 [1897]) was particularly concerned with modern aspects of society and their negative effects on one's sense of belonging and direction or hope within a larger set of relationships and social structure. He viewed anomic and egoistic suicides as having "kindred ties," with anomie leaving individual passions without a "check-rein" and egoism leaving people without meaning (p. 258). Anomie "disorients and disconcerts" while egoism "agitates and exasperates" (p. 382). Both were products of the modern society, and Durkheim argued that they explained the three- to fivefold increase in suicide during the half-century preceding his book's publication in 1897.

Anomie has been interpreted by most scholars as normlessness together with failed expectations. Rapid and uncontrolled social change, according to Durkheim, produced a crisis leading to anomie and vulnerability to suicide. LaCapra (2001) sees anomie as caused by "runaway

change" at the social level. Anomie stems from, in Tomasi's (2000) interpretation of Durkheim, boundless and unsatisfied moral needs. Parsons
(1960, p. 124) defined norms as "generalized patterns of expectation"
that differ across groups within a social system. Anomie would thus be a
breakdown of expectations and hope, a breakdown of norms. Mestrovic
(1992) discussed anomie as unsatisfied human desires, noting that entire
collectives will experience this if their expectations, set by a more powerful majority "in-group," cannot be met because of their "out-group"
status. "New hopes constantly awake, only to be deceived, leaving a trail
of weariness and disillusionment behind them" (Durkheim, 1951, p. 271
[1897]). Rapid social change thus leads to demoralization and the inability to meet new expectations. Anomie, together with its close relative
alienation, are social conditions leading to a perturbed mental state.

It turns out that, from the data available, Western cultures continue to
have higher suicide rates than non-Western ones. "Westernizing" cultures
in the midst of high-speed social change generally have very high suicide
rates among their youth. Examining quality of life and suicide across
43 nations, Lester (1996b) found a positive correlation between the two
with the most predictive quality of life variables to be health, wealth, and
education. These are central features of Western society. In a review of the
literature on the relationship between suicide and unmet expectations,
Baumeister (1990) found that suicides are higher among those whose
higher-than-average expectations were met with poor outcomes. Suicide
rates are higher among economically prosperous countries, countries
or even states with higher standards of living, countries with "better"
climates, and in North America in the late spring/early summer when
the weather is improving. Rates are higher among college students than
their peers not in college, and among students with above average grades
whose grades have dropped. A drop in the standard of living, seen in an
increase in suicide in the U.S. during periods of economic depression or
recession, is a social suicide risk factor. Baumeister found that setbacks
and downward turns were common in suicides. Recently divorced or
separated people have higher suicide rates (Breault & Kposowa, 2000), as
do widowed men. So do persons with deteriorating health or work situations. Again, these all have more to do with perturbation than suicide.

Egoism, or social alienation, has likewise received empirical support. While Durkheim argued that religion was a prophylactic against
suicide, especially the Jewish and Catholic faiths, studies have found
that it is a person's integration into religious groups that decreases suicide risk among those religiously inclined rather than type of religion
per se or even personal faith in a god (Pescosolido, 1990). He believed
that a strongly integrated society "forbids" suicides because individuals
are at its service, committed to working for each other (p. 209). This
may explain the success of Napoleon's warning to his soldiers referred
to earlier. An integrated society provides an individual "solidarity with

collective existence" (p. 374). Measures of social disintegration are found to be positively associated with suicide rates from around the world (Lester, 1996b). Egoistic suicide, according to Durkheim, was caused by "excessive individualism" (1951, p. 209 [1897]). It is interesting that a prominent psychologist has recently attributed American individualism to being the major factor in what he calls the current epidemic of depression (Seligman, 2000).

The sociology of suicide is thus founded on Durkheim. Most sociological research on the topic has continued to be statistical with a focus on demographic correlates. Steven Stack (2000a, 2000b), the most prolific researcher on the sociology of suicide over the last two decades, conducted a systematic review of the sociological research on suicide. The Durkheimian notion of poor social integration and suicide is generally supported. Modernization as economic development is associated with an increase in suicide, likely related to poverty or economic loss, while other variables such as increases in telephones, education, and urbanization have received mixed support. A curvilinear effect is found for urbanization, with an initial increase in suicides followed by a plateau. Rural suicides are higher than urban suicides in the U.S. Age and suicide are correlated where a particular age group has fewer social and/or material resources. Marriage is still generally protective, and suicides rates are higher for divorced men. Religion, as mentioned earlier, is protective when it involves active integration with a religious community. Islam has been identified as a particular case example of high religious community integration and low suicide. Major wars show lower suicide rates, but the variables accounting for this may be lowered unemployment and alcoholism during these times. Yet people may feel a greater sense of national belonging during a war, Durkheim's collective sentiments. Male suicide rates continue to be higher than female rates in most countries, and this gap has been widening due to an overall slight decrease in female suicide. There is little agreement on an interpretation of this sex difference. A general inverse relationship is observed between social/economic class and suicide; however certain high-class occupations demonstrate a higher suicide rate (e.g., dentists, physicians).

So is suicide decided upon as an act of free will? Is it a consciously rational decision, based on some possibly irrational judgments? Or is it determined by a mental illness, a "chemical imbalance"? As indicated earlier, there are no chemical imbalances in mental disorders (Angell, 2011b). As we have seen, the view of suicide has changed over time from free will to determinism. Suicide as caused by sin or illegal conduct to being caused by a mental disease. Suicide today is seen as a result of a mental disorder and multiple suicide risk factors. It is deterministic. "He didn't want to kill himself, he had major depressive disorder." Yet, as pointed out by Münster and Broz (2015), there is still a *tension* of agency in suicidology. This is where suicide is seen as intentional, such as in my definition of suicide at the beginning of this chapter as an act of willfully taking one's own life, and as caused by forces external to the individual such as depression, genetics, gender, or stress. Münster and Broz see some of the tension of agency in suicide being viewed as a "bad" death, with bad coming from the willful intention to end one's life. They also see tension between the notions of intentionality and responsibility. While intention may have been there, the person was not fully responsible. Lester and Stack (2015, p. 324) see suicide from an agentic view, as a "dramatic act or performance, scripted and staged by the suicidal individual." Durkheim believed that suicide was inflicted onto people by society, that is was a social fact. Yet Jaworski (2014, p. 189) cites Judith Butler regarding agency: "Our acts are not self-generated, but conditioned. We are at once acted upon and acting." So suicide might be intentionally acted out, but influenced by external factors. Depression makes me hate myself, so suicide may be a welcome cultural idea. Yet suicide remains a mystery, and the tension of agency also remains so.

3 Social Epidemics

I once wrote that in order to understand how the idea of suicide works, we need to examine how ideas are spread in a society, how they become an acceptable option for a group of people or an individual (Kral, 1994). This will help us understand how the idea of suicide can do the same. In this chapter we will look at this in the form of social epidemics or what some call mass hysteria. Charles Mackay wrote a classic nineteenth-century book called *Memoirs of Extraordinary Popular Delusions and the Madness of Crowds* (Mackay, 1852). In this book he covers many group actions such as witch-hunts, lynch mobs, fads, fortune-telling, popular slang phrases, investment schemes, pilgrimages, mesmerism, and even wars. He wrote in the preface:

> In reading the history of nations, we find that whole communities suddenly fix their minds upon one object, and go mad in its pursuit; that millions of people become simultaneously impressed with one delusion, and run after it, till their attention is caught by some new folly more captivating than the first. We see one nation suddenly seized, from its highest to its lowest members, with a fierce desire of military glory; another as suddenly becoming crazed upon a religious scruple; and neither of them recovering its senses until it has shed rivers of blood and sowed a harvest of groans and tears, to be reaped by its posterity. . . . Men, it has been well said, think in herds; it will be seen that they go mad in herds, while they only recover their senses slowly, and one by one.
>
> (pp. xix–xx)

Contagion and imitation are seen across most human endeavors (Levy & Nail, 1993). The game of cricket became popular with countries closely tied to England, and Kaufman and Patterson (2005) found diffusion to work through elites or cultural entrepreneurs spreading interest in it. Murder-suicides often appear to be imitations. Hush Puppy shoes became extremely popular in 1995 after some young people in

New York City started wearing them, and they were not popular previously. Then two fashion designers used those shoes to sell haute couture, and suddenly they became so popular that they were being sold in every mall in North America (Gladwell, 2000). Financial contagion has been identified (Allen & Gale, 2000; Kodres & Pritsker, 2002), which can be promoted through globalization (Calvo & Mendoza, 2000). Personal preferences account for the social contagion of technological innovation (Burt, 1987). Moods are contagious (Neumann & Strack, 2000). Group norms for the social contagion of binge eating have been found (Crandall, 1988). It is, of course, well known that the buying of products is contagious (Iyengar, Bulte, & Valente, 2011). School shootings are contagious (Goode, 2018). Prescribing behavior among doctors is contagious (Christakis & Fowler, 2011). Memory can be contagious (Roediger, Meade, & Bergman, 2001). Even martyrdom was "extraordinarily contagious" (Smith, 1997, p. 18). There is thus no reason to believe that suicide is not also contagious. Humans are fundamentally imitative of each other.

Epidemics and pandemics have existed since the fifth century BCE, and 50 are discussed in a book by Hays (2005). These have been diseases spread across large numbers of people. Rosenberg (1992) refers to epidemics as contagious, where diseases are "transportable." There was yellow fever, cholera, tuberculosis, AIDS, and many more. There can also be social epidemics through what has been called the mass mind or mass psychology (Blackman & Walkerdine, 2001). It is based on collective behavior, what Smelser (2011, p. 5) defines as "mobilization on the basis of a belief which redefines social action." It is guided by beliefs that are communicated across people that become action. This communication can be in the form of gestures, signs, face-to-face talking, the mass media, and so on. They may be fashion cycles, financial booms, or panics. Outbreaks of mass hysteria based on contagion of ideas and actions have been with us across all time, it appears. Evans and Bartholomew (2009) describe 340 social epidemics or outbreaks, incidents of extraordinary collective behavior, over many countries and centuries.

In the book *The June Bug: A Study of Hysterical Contagion*, Kerckoff and Back (1968) report on a contagious reaction to an apparent bug bite. This took place in 1962 in a small town in the southern U.S. called Strongsville. In the news, it was written,

> During the past three weeks a number of the 200 employees had been stricken with a mysterious illness, apparently caused by an insect bite. Today about ten women and one man were stricken. Several were admitted to the hospital for treatment and observation. Company officials say they are fumigating the building.

This plant had 965 workers, and it manufactured women's clothing. When interviewed by the authors, one woman said,

> I was working and I felt a sting on my arm and I looked down and had a place on it. I scratched it, and my arm began to get numb. I got nauseated and they took me to the first aid room.

Another person indicated, "That is actually what I believe it was—an insect bite. I could see the girls as they fell over. I saw one girl's head draw back. She had convulsions." Sixty-two employees were seen by physicians, 57 because of this insect bite. Half the people interviewed attributed the symptoms to an insect bite. The others thought it was something else or they were puzzled. The spread of the insect bite symptoms spread rapidly and just as rapidly diminished. Most of the cases occurred during a two-day period. Experts looking into this phenomenon reached the conclusion that it was nothing but anxiety. They found no evidence that any insect was present that could have caused the symptoms. They also cite the definition from Grosser, Polansky, and Lippittas (1951, p. 115) as

> a social interaction in which a recipient's behavior changes to become 'more like' that of another person, and where this change has occurred in a social interaction in which the 'initiator' (other person) has not communicated intent to influence the behavior of the recipient.

Hysteria was, and some would say still is, what Showalter (1997, p. 9) called a "cultural symptom of anxiety and stress." Hysteria was very contagious over a century ago. It was a symptom pool, a culturally determined template of how people manifest symptoms (Shorter, 1992). The word comes from the Greek word for uterus, *hystera*. Some believe the concept was used in the Hippocratic texts of the fifth century, but the term first appeared in English in 1615 and French in 1658 (Micale, 1989). It was referred to as a disease after 1731, and a London medical journal first referred to hysteria in 1801 (Micale, 1995). From the mid- to the late nineteenth century, French and German physicians saw hysteria as an innate neuropathic disorder. Charcot, the famous French psychiatrist in the late 1800s, saw it as hereditary and organic. During his time the major paradigm was that of organic nervous disease. There were many nerve doctors around (Shorter, 1992). Charcot distinguished hysteria from epilepsy and all other mental disorders (Didi-Huberman, 2003). It was Freud who turned hysteria into a psychological issue, caused by the repression of traumatic memories that were unconsciously converted into somatic symptoms (Micale, 1989). A psychological paradigm over an organic one became popular after the 1880s (Shorter, 1992). The history of psychiatry was founded on hysteria, and psychoanalysis began as a theory of hysteria (Micale, 1995).

Sirois (1982) described what he called hysterical epidemics through history. There were many of them. One was called the dancing manias of the fourteenth century. It appeared in northern Germany and spread rapidly. People would go into an ecstatic frenzy, throwing themselves on the ground with convulsive movements and twitching, or they would clap their hands while naked. This involved groups of a few hundred people. Historian Andrew Scull (2009, p. 93) writes of hysteria: "The fits, the paralyses, the choking, the tearing of hair, the remarkable emotional instability, all with no obvious organic substrate. . . . Was hysteria 'real' or fictitious, somatic or psychopathological?" In the 1600s the symptoms included belching, striving to vomit, choking, laughing or weeping, absurd talking, and convulsive motions. Much of this was associated with witchcraft, as young girls would present such symptoms and many times older women were accused of casting spells.

Scull (2009) presents a case of a young girl in 1602 who received very angry words from an old woman. The girl presented with dances and prancing, slow movements, strange breathing, odd vocalizations, paralyses, trances, tics, spasms, and loud cries. The old woman was accused of witchcraft. Girls presented as having had spells cast on them in Salem in the late 1600s, and would manifest motor symptoms such as arms flailing, head jerking, leaping and running, violent jerking of body parts, fainting, barking like a dog, and crying out. This started with two young girls, and then spread to other young girls, who named three older women as having bewitched them. The three women were committed to a jail in Boston. It then spread even more, and more older women and some men were arrested. Demos (2008) believes that these symptoms followed a well-known script, a cultural idiom, known in the Anglo-American world. Witch-hunting was high in Poland in the late 1600s, extensive in Germany between 1627 and 1632, in Scotland between 1590 and 1660, and in Virginia from 1626 to 1706. The peak of witch-hunting in Europe was in the years 1580 to 1650 (Demos, 2008). Harris (1974) estimated that 500,000 people in Europe were convicted of witchcraft and burned to death between the fifteenth and seventeenth centuries. Most people accused of witchcraft were middle-aged women who were contentious and abrasive, and who were poorer than most others. Many of the afflicted accusers were teenage girls. Historians John Demos (2008, p. 37) and Boyer and Nissenbaum (1974) called witch-hunting a contagious mass hysteria, noting that, "Occasionally, witch-hunts would spread from one place to another, as if by a kind of contagion." At least 156 people were accused of witchcraft in 1692 in Salem, and 20 were executed (Baker, 2015). This was the first time that children were called upon to testify in criminal cases, as children were doing the accusing. Seventy-eight percent of those accused in Salem were women (Dennis & Reis, 2015). Demos estimates that 50,000–100,000 "witches" were executed around the world, and it was mostly women accusing women of witchcraft. All this started in Europe during the sixteenth and seventeenth centuries with schoolchildren acting in bizarre ways. The first known case took place in 1566 in a Catholic orphanage school in Amsterdam, where children had strange fits and compulsions, arms and legs seizing in violent spasms or the children acting like cats. People thought the children were possessed by demons and exorcists were brought in (Bartholomew & Rickard, 2014).

Hysteria

In the eighteenth century in France hysteria was seen as difficulty breathing, sleeplessness, toothache, immobility, and later paralysis (Scull, 2009). Paralysis was uncommon before 1800, but it increased to a large degree after (Shorter, 1992). Hysterics "suffered from a bewildering variety of both physical and psychological complaints" (Fancher, 1973, p. 34). Breuer and Freud (1957 [1895]) published a major book on hysteria. They present cases of their patients. The symptoms included eccentricity, impulsiveness, emotionality, deceitfulness, coquettishness (flirtatious), and hypersexuality. Their most famous patient, Anna O or Bertha Pappenheim, had quite a number and variety of symptoms, which included paraphasia or the production of unintended syllables, words, or phrases, and a loss to find words, a squint, disturbances of vision, paralysis in right upper extremity, paresis (loss of voluntary movement) of neck muscles, sleepwalking, sleeplessness, headache, throwing cushions at people, tearing buttons off her clothes, not being able to recognize people, refusing to eat, occasional deafness, hallucinations of snakes, outbreaks of anger, spasms of coughing. She created quite a scene. The symptoms of hysteria were quite varied and emotional.

As Micale (1995, p. 111) writes, hysteria is a "disease whose essence lies in imitating other diseases." He adds that hysteria was easily spread by suggestion and imitation, models being provided in novels, films, and journalism. He notes that in the nineteenth century people were more likely to somaticize their anxieties, as psychological processes were not well known. The vast majority of hysterics were women. As Showalter (1997, p. 8) noted, "Being hysterical means being overemotional, irresponsible, and feminine." Scull (2009, p. 7) writes about this feminism: "Might it constitute an unspoken idiom of protest, a symbolic voice for the silenced sex, who were forbidden to verbalize their discontents, and so created a language of the body?" Showalter shows that feminist critics see hysteria as a form of silencing. She notes that 80% of people with chronic fatigue syndrome are women, and more than 90% of people who report recovered memories of child sexual abuse and who were diagnosed with multiple personality disorder were women. Women outnumber men in all cases of unexplained illness.

But hysteria has disappeared. What happened to it? Women no longer produce such great, theatrical symptoms. How does a mental disorder disappear? Ian Hacking (2002) wrote a book about another mental disorder, the fugue, that appeared out of nowhere in France in the early twentieth century and then suddenly disappeared. He proposed that many mental disorders need what he called an ecological niche. They can only flourish in a particular environment. They need cultural models of experience and expression that are copied, what are called cultural idioms of distress, and they need a medical community that will recognize the disorder. Hacking referred to such mental distress as a transient mental illness. A number of mental disorders may be transient. Idioms of distress change over time, as does the professional view of various mental disorders. Shorter (1992) refers to diseases of fashion, spread through doctors, the public, and the media, and what he calls hypersuggestibility. Elaine Showalter (1997) has three requirements for hysterical epidemics to exist: enthusiastic professionals; unhappy, vulnerable patients; and cultural environments that support this. Some believe that hysteria has become other disorders, including anorexia nervosa, multiple personality disorder, and fatigue syndromes. As Scull (2009, p. 6) indicated, "The malady seems to change its shape and its forms over the centuries." Bollas (2000) believes that hysterics are now people with borderline personality disorder. Having treated a number of such patients, they may be theatrical, but I would disagree. Schowalter sees anorexia and bulimia as hysterical, psychogenic epidemics. She also sees chronic fatigue syndrome, Gulf War syndrome, recovered memory, multiple personality disorder, satanic ritual abuse, and alien abduction as hysterical epidemics. Showalter thinks hysteria is more contagious today than in the past. The psychiatric diagnoses today most closely associated with hysteria are somatic symptom and related disorders and histrionic personality disorder (American Psychiatric Association, 2013). Multiple personality disorder, now called dissociative identity disorder, has almost disappeared. It was a medical fad (Best, 2006). It was very popular in the 1980s, and most patients were women. Before the 1980s it was rare. It was primarily a North American phenomenon, basically a culture-bound syndrome (Wenegrat, 2001), another transient mental illness, like hysteria and the fugue.

Phoon (1982) described outbreaks of mass hysteria at several workplaces in Singapore. In the first case, where most of the workers were women, one worker started screaming and then fainted. Other women were affected the same way, 97 of them. They screamed, struggled, and were even violent. The workers affected expressed feelings of unexplained fear and being cold, numb, or dizzy. In another factory, a woman screamed and collapsed to the floor. Soon others were doing this. Phoon indicates that the onset was sudden, that it spread quickly, and the outbreak subsided on its own within about a week. All affected workers were female. Colligan and Murphy (1982) reviewed 23 cases of mass psychogenic illness in work settings, and found that of 1,223 people who enacted the illness, 89% were female. They thought these women experienced greater "off the job" stressors, which made them more susceptible. Kerckoff (1982) thought that women are more often found in jobs that are repetitive, boring, and restrictive, and that these poor work conditions make them vulnerable. Colligan and Murphy found that many of these people had a history of absenteeism from work; were bored; were feeling pressure from work; were experiencing physical stressors such as poor lighting, excessive noise, temperature variations, foul odors, and dust in the air; and had poor labor-management relations.

Sirois (1982) identified five types of hysterical epidemics. There is the sudden onset explosive type, where symptoms appear rapidly, involve many people, and are usually short lived. The insect bite epidemic would be an example of this. The second type is explosive with a prodromal stage, a gradual build-up of tension followed by an explosive outbreak. A third type is cumulative, where fewer than ten people are involved and transmission takes longer, two weeks to a month. A fourth type is rebound, where cases appear followed by a second wave of people taking on symptoms. These outbreaks last one to two months. The fifth type is the large diffuse outbreak, which is not restricted to specific groups, and there are rebounds. A large number of people are involved.

Fads have always been with us. Best (2006) writes that we are prone to picking up fads because we believe in progress, perfectibility, revolution, and rationality, making us open to new ideas and behaviors. He mentioned the hula hoop as one fad that emerged in the late 1950s in North America. Every kid had to have one. Then interest in it stopped, and nobody had one anymore. Then there are fads that stay, like the wristwatch. When it was first introduced back around 1915, there was much debate. Men did not want to replace their pocket watches, a very male attribute. *The New York Times* quoted a delegate at the National Retail Jewelers' Association conference, saying, "There's some excuse for a woman wearing her watch on her wrist . . . but a man . . . has plenty of pockets" (Best, 2006, p. 6). Then the wristwatch took off among men, and it is still extremely popular even with everyone having a cell phone that tells the time. Best (2006) mentions sociologist Emory Bogardus who, between 1915 and 1924, asked 100 people each year to name five fads taking place at that time. Most fads did not last long enough to make the list more than once, and only a few made it across three years. One of these was men's wristwatches.

Fads come in all shapes and sizes. Fashion is one common fad. Janney (1941) found that college women took on clothing fads in a systematic manner after initiation by young women who were members of prestige-bearing cliques and leaders. There are always fashion fads like bobbed hair among women in the 1920s, miniskirts in the 1970s, Velcro sneakers in the 1980s, Cabbage Patch dolls in 1983–1985, and the Atkins diet in 2003–2004. Hempel (2014) writes how the "selfie" became a social epidemic. The type of dog one has can be a fad, as Herzog (2006) found rapid and transient large-scale increases in the popularity of specific dog breeds. Steep decreases in registration for the breeds immediately followed the jumps in popularity. A global fad has become Facebook (Ugander, Backstrom, Marlow, & Kleinberg, 2012). Hoffman and Bailey (1992) see many forms of psychotherapy as fads. The pharmaceutical industry promotes medical fads; psychoanalysis was a fad, as was frontal lobotomy, as is attention-deficit hyperactivity disorder (ADHD) in adults, as is the diagnosis of post-traumatic stress disorder (PTSD) (Paris, 2013).

Other fads have included skateboards, bubble gum, Silly Putty, Scrabble, and the Frisbee (Sann, 1967). Sann (1967) reported that the dean of the graduate school at University of Southern California had his students collect information on fads. They found about 3,000 of them, and most disappeared within six months to a year. The dean said,

> As soon as most fads are widely adopted, they no longer attract attention and they are dropped. Another factor helps to explain fads as a current phenomenon. They flourish only in social environments in which people are looking forward and seeking progress by trying out new things and ideas. In countries tied down by customs, rituals, and the like, fads have no standing. In countries whose eyes are forward looking, fads are adopted by the many, and even at the hand of their devotees they are quickly discarded for a newer, and, if possible, more glamorous object.
>
> (Sann, 1967, p. 1)

Mass Outbreaks

Many cases of mass hysteria have been published. One case is from a girl's boarding school in Nigeria (Ali-Gombe, Guthrie, & McDermott, 1996). A 16-year-old schoolgirl developed weakness in her lower limbs and was unable to walk properly. She was admitted to a hospital. Within a day, 22 other girls developed similar symptoms and were taken to the hospital. No reason for their symptoms could be found. The school was closed, and it re-opened after a few weeks. In Santa Monica, California, student performers came down with symptoms soon after an assembly began (Small, Propper, Randolph, & Eth, 1991). Students complained of headaches, dizziness, weakness, abdominal pain, and nausea. The symptoms spread quickly and affected 247 students. The auditorium was evacuated. The next day it was announced that no fumes or toxic materials were found. It was described as mass hysteria. In a North Carolina high school, adolescent students developed what looked like spasms, seizures, and hyperventilation (Roach & Langley, 2004). All ten students were girls. One student started with having seizure-like attacks, and over the next few weeks the other girls developed the same symptoms. Some of their symptoms included dizziness, headache, numbness, shortness of breath, and tingling. Physicians suggested panic attacks, depression, or anxiety in four students. All diagnostic tests came out as normal. Again, mass hysteria. In India, a 31-member family displayed aches and pains, tiredness, indigestion, insomnia, and work problems, which were associated with mass hysteria (Mattoo, Gupta, Lobana, & Bedi, 2002). There was another case of insect bite hysteria in a textile plant in the U.S.

Mass hysteria has often been seen in Africa. Belief in supernaturalism and witchcraft is behind many of these cases (Kokota, 2011). One case was seen in a primary school in Uganda. In one school, a girl thought she was being attacked by demons and began shouting, running amok, fighting, biting, and crying (Nakalawa, Musisi, Kinyanda, & Okello, 2010). It was difficult to restrain her. Several other students then had similar symptoms, adding up to 54 students. No medical problems. Another case was in a secondary boarding school in Zambia, Africa (Dhadphale & Shaikh, 1983). A 17-year-old girl in one class started with uncontrollable laughter and then began twitching and reciting poems loudly and became euphoric and confused. Four other girls manifested the same behaviors, and the next day more girls and a few boys were affected, and they caused severe damage to school property such that the police were called. The situation in the school was described as explosive. They suspected that food was the cause. The food was checked and found to be fine, and no organic illness was found. In rural Mexico, adolescents in a female religious boarding school developed symptoms of having a fever, diarrhea, nausea, and pain when walking (Zavala, 2010). Five hundred and twelve students were affected out of about 4,000 students. Physicians ruled out any medical problems.

A case was described by Balaratnasinggam and Janca (2006, p. 171):

> At Virgin Blue terminal of Melbourne's Tullamarine Airport, a worker at the news agency complained of feeling ill. Within an hour, another two reported feeling of being unwell, albeit with different symptoms. Soon, 47 people, mostly airport staff, were reporting dizziness, nausea, vomiting, and respiratory problems with more than 40 taken to a hospital by ambulance. Paramedics treated others at the scene. The symptoms remitted quickly in the majority. The terminal was, however, plunged into full emergency mode, forcing its evacuation, and subsequent closure for 8 hours. More than 60 Virgin Blue flights were cancelled, 14,000 people were stranded, and the cost ran into the millions. Two months later and after an investigation by Victoria's Emergency Services Commissioner, no causes for these events had been found and no clear explanation has been offered.

An outbreak was seen among high school students in Taiwan (Cheng-Sheng, Cheng-Fang, Lin, & Pingchen, 2000). The first student began to have intense difficulty breathing and swallowing, followed by dizziness, fainting, and verbal outbursts. A number of female classmates repeated this behavior. They were all brought to the emergency room of a local hospital. Again, no medical problems. A group of about 500 seventh and eighth grade students were traveling on an exchange trip from Quebec City to their town in Ontario and stopped at the train station in Montreal to change trains (Moffatt, 1982). One 14-year-old girl began to feel dizzy and fainted. Very rapidly, six other girls fainted and many began to feel weak and dizzy with symptoms of headache, shakiness, tingling in arms and legs, and abdominal pain. Railway police were notified, and 13 girls were rushed by ambulance to a hospital. At the hospital they determined this to be epidemic hysteria. Finally, the McMartin sexual abuse case has been described as a case of mass hysteria (Fukurai, Butler, & Krooth, 1994). In 1984, a TV station in Los Angeles broke a story of alleged child molestation at a preschool and reported that it might be linked to child pornography rings and the sex industry. Workers at the preschool were accused, and before their trial about 90% of residents in Los Angeles County believed that they were guilty. The trial began in 1987 and there was massive publicity about it. Almost 400 children who attended the school were interviewed, and 41 were listed as victims. The children reported seeing witches fly, traveling in a hot air balloon, and being taken in underground tunnels. One child identified a famous actor as one of the abusers. This was the longest and costliest trial in American history. The accused were acquitted, as no evidence was found. One of the children as an adult retracted the allegations of abuse. This day care sex scandal was called an epidemic caused by contagion by Frances (2013), mimicking the Salem witch trials. Another case of mass hysteria, what Demos (2008) called a witch hunt.

In 1938 Orson Welles and the Mercury Theatre were going to have a dramatization of H. G. Wells' *The War of the Worlds* over the CBS radio station. A bulletin from Intercontinental Radio News announced that a professor had observed several explosions on the planet Mars, and then that a huge cylinder, perhaps a meteor, landed in New Jersey. An end of the cylinder was being unscrewed and monsters were coming out with bear faces and snake eyes. It was announced that 7,000 guardsmen had been defeated by the aliens, and more cylinders were landing. There was a nationwide panic, primarily in New Jersey. The monsters were Martians. Many people were going to police stations, and 20 families in New Jersey reported they were under a gas attack. In Trenton, New Jersey, public communications systems were tied up by callers panicking about the invasion. Cities were being evacuated. Orson Welles regretted his action the next day to the press. Lawsuits were filed against CBS, but none were legally proved. A mass hysteria about Martians (Chaplin, 2015).

Dawes (2014) called mass hysteria a contagious conversion disorder. In 1993 at a school in Thailand a girl in grade three had a strange look in her eyes, and she told people that she had been taken over by a spirit. She entered into trances. Soon 32 classmates were exhibiting fits with headaches and dizziness. A public prayer ceremony was organized to get rid of demons. Psychiatrists attributed the symptoms to stress. In 1999 in Antwerp, Belgium, 33 students were rushed to a hospital after drinking cans of Coca-Cola. Their symptoms were headache, nausea, stomach pain, breathing problems, and dizziness. Doctors found nothing wrong with them. In 2002 in a rural high school in North Carolina, ten girls had strange seizures with fainting, shortness of breath, headaches, lightheadedness, muscle twitching and jerking, tingling, and numbness. Five years later the same thing happened in a high school in Virginia, with an outbreak of twitching arms and legs, headaches, and dizziness. In 2004 in Orissa, India, at least a dozen girls began acting like cats. Native healers were summoned. These and many other cases of mass hysteria in schools have been described by Bartholomew and Rickard (2014).

Stahl (1982) reported on a case of odor-sniffing hysteria. This happened at a data processing center of a major mid-western university in the U.S. It took place over two days. Thirty-five workers smelled a "mystery gas" and became ill with headaches, hyperventilation, nausea, vomiting, burning eyes, and fainting. Ten workers were taken to the hospital's emergency room. The next day, within an hour of starting work the symptoms recurred, and the building was again closed. Workers returned to the emergency room. The day after that, a physician from the emergency room met with the workers and told them all was now fine. He did not tell them that all medical tests were negative. Only one worker subsequently hyperventilated and was sent home.

A number of writers have speculated on the phenomenon of mass hysteria. Most find it to be poorly understood. Balaratnasinggam and Janca (2006) found that most of these epidemics are started by an actual event, and a common trigger is odor, like the gasoline smell in two of our cases. They indicate that mass hysteria was seen as motor hysteria in the Middle Ages, and during the Industrial Revolution it had symptoms of breathlessness, nausea, headache, dizziness, and weakness, which we saw in many of the cases. Wessely (1987) believes that there are two syndromes in mass hysteria. The first he calls mass anxiety hysteria, with symptoms of abdominal pain, chest tightness, dizziness, fainting, headache, hyperventilation, nausea, and palpitation. The second is mass motor hysteria, with symptoms of numbness, blindness, paralysis, or fits. Wessely has many of these epidemics associated with sociocultural stress. Freedman (1982) describes principles by which psychogenic illness contagion operates. It first begins with only a few people and then spreads. There is no known physical cause of the illness, although the people may have been under some stress. The stress is not enough to cause the illness. Also, people do not try to purposefully influence others. The people actually believe that they are sick.

Olkinuora (1984) identified predisposing factors to mass hysteria in work settings as boredom, pressure to produce, physical stressors, poor labor-management relations, poor interpersonal communication, and lack of support. There is no agreement on identifying features or personality characteristics of people who have such symptoms. Boss (1997) found that the most frequent settings where such epidemics took place are schools, places of employment, and small communities. A number occur in factories, and most of the school outbreaks take place in the classroom. While most of the people exhibiting this behavior are female, most of the people who are exposed to the triggering factor but who do not develop symptoms are also female. These are otherwise healthy people. Outbreaks in non-Western cultures often take place in schools where Western concepts are taught, ones that are contrary to those taught at home. Contagion takes place when people are physically close together. More than one-third of symptoms include nausea, vomiting, headaches, and dizziness. Relapses are common. Boss (1997, p. 240) notes, "These outbreaks are frequently explosive in nature, with many people becoming ill in a short period and their symptoms resolving before an investigation can be initiated."

Fleischer (2011) has written about mass hysterias. He describes a dancing plague that took place in France in 1518. One woman began dancing on a street in Strasbourg, France. She did not stop for days and was joined by 34 people within a week and 400 by the end of the month. There has been no explanation for this. In Mattoon, Illinois, in 1944, someone reported smelling a strong odor. This woman said the smell got stronger and she began to lose feeling in her legs. This got out on the news. Over the next few weeks the police received over a dozen reports of a bad smell in people's houses. Nothing was found. The police ended up getting many false alarms, and then suddenly it all stopped. In 1962, there was a laughter epidemic in the U.K. It took place in an all-girls school. Three young girls broke into laughter in the middle of the day and could not stop. Their laughter was uncontrollable, and it was contagious. Soon 95 of the school's 159 students were laughing, many to the point of crying. It went on for hours, and some girls had multiple fits of laughing randomly for up to two weeks. The school closed for three days. In Portugal in 2006 a very popular soap opera on television had an episode where a potentially killer virus infects a school. Within days of the episode, more than 300 children in 14 different schools were reporting the symptoms from the show: rashes, dizziness, and trouble breathing.

Another laughter epidemic took place in a Malaysian classroom, where a young girl started flailing and screaming, falling on the floor, and cursing the principal. One student started to laugh, and then more students began laughing. Some were laughing for days, and soon thousands were laughing and the school was forced to close for weeks (Bartholomew & Rickard, 2014).

Freeman-Longo and Blanchard (1998) refer to sexual abuse in America as an epidemic of the twenty-first century. There is the opioid epidemic

(Marcovitz, 2018), the obesity epidemic (Bellisari, 2013; Cohen, 2014), the depression epidemic (Wakefield & Demazeux, 2016), the epidemic of violence in America (Gilligan, 1996), the narcissism/self-admiration epidemic (Twenge & Campbell, 2009), the bullying epidemic (Blumen, 2010), the ADHD epidemic (Wedge, 2015), the psychosomatic disorders epidemic (Sarno, 2006), and the autism epidemic (Goldberg, 2014). Most of these epidemics are in America and not elsewhere, so it is cultural. Mass shootings appear to be contagious (Servitje & Nixon, 2016), as do police shootings (Casper, 2016).

Suicide pacts also exist, where there is a common agreement between two or more persons that they will kill themselves together. Most pacts do not involve young lovers, and 71% are over the age of 50. These deaths appear to be carefully planned, and the relationship among the members is usually intense (Rosen, 1981). Family suicide pacts are much less common, but they have taken place. Suicide pacts usually take place during January and February, unlike single suicides that take place mostly in May and June. The motives of suicide pacts are not clear. Pacts have been more common in Japan, where they are called *shinju* (Rosen, 1981). I was familiar with one pact suicide of a young couple in a small city in which I lived in Canada. What was interesting is that a former girlfriend of the boy from the suicide pact came forward and said that he had tried to convince her to do the same.

Suicide clusters are also well known, when suicides take place within a group and setting within a short time of each other, usually between one week and over one year. Suicide clusters are known in institutional settings such as psychiatric hospitals, schools, prisons, and military commands, as well as in Indigenous communities, work community settings, and the general population, mostly involving young people (Bechtold, 1988; Boyce, 2011; Exeter & Boyle, 2007; Gould, Wallenstein, & Davidson, 1989; Gould, 2001; Hanssens, 2007; Haw, Hawton, Niedzwiedz, & Platt, 2013; Niedzwiedz, Haw, Hawton, & Platt, 2014; Niezen, 2009; Phillips & Carstensen, 1986; Rubenstein, 1983). Imitative suicide in prisons has been found (McKenzie & Keane, 2007). Cluster suicide may be more common among institutionalized youth (Hazell, 1993).

Suicide has appeared in clusters throughout history (Colt, 1991). Niedzwiedz et al. (2014) identify two types of cluster: mass, where suicides occur closer in time than would be expected by chance, and point, which is suicide or suicidal behavior localized in both time and place, often occurring in a small community or institution. The Centers for Disease Control has published a plan for the prevention of suicide clusters in communities (Gould et al., 1989), and more recently, in collaboration with other agencies (e.g., NIMH, Office of the Surgeon General, World Health Organization), guidelines for the reporting of suicide for the media in an attempt to offset contagion effects (Centers for Disease Control and Prevention 2002). Haw et al. (2013) found that adolescents and young adults are at highest risk for suicide clusters, with other risk factors including being male and having direct involvement with another cluster victim, a past history of self-harm, and current drug/alcohol abuse. The method of suicide is culturally scripted for particular communities or geographic regions cross-sectionally (Farberow, 1975; Kral & Walsh, 2000), and the most popular methods can also change over time within one population (Chotai, Renberg, & Jacobsson, 1999). Indeed, illness roles tend to be scripted differently in different societies, and they are contagious (Wenegrat, 2001). Suicide has been found to run in families, and it appears to be a better social learning rather than a genetic explanation that suicide begets suicide (Brent et al., 2003; Qin, Agerbo, & Mortensen, 2003). Can suicide be seen as something of a viable option, an acceptable form of behavior? Common sense is a cultural system, according to Geertz (1983), with things as they are, the ways things go.

Suicide clusters took place in early Greece and Rome, there were early Christian martyrs, and suicide clusters were found in the Middle Ages. A number of suicide clusters took place in Russia. Suicide by fire, self-immolation, has been copied around the world. Teenagers have made cluster suicides. Clusters are the result of contagion (Blasco-Fontecilla, 2012). Haw et al. (2013) indicate that there are two types of cluster suicides, mass clusters that are media-driven after the reporting of suicides, and point clusters that take place in a small geographical area over a relatively brief period of time, and are driven by contagion, imitation, and suggestion. There has been a clustering of teenage suicides after television news stories about suicide (Phillips & Carstensen, 1986). There have been waves of postal suicides and shootings that had the term coined "going postal." School shootings have been copied.

Mass suicides are the simultaneous suicide of all members of a group or sect. Mass suicides have taken place throughout history, typically to avoid persecution (Farberow, 1975; Jamison, 1999; Szasz, 1999). For example, 3,000–4,000 German Jews killed themselves due to deportation between 1941 and 1943. During the weeks before German surrender, "suicide became almost a routine phenomenon in Germany" and it became an epidemic in 1945 (Goeschel, 2009, p. 156). Mancinelli, Comparelli, Girardi, and Tatarelli (2002) describe two types of mass suicide: self-induced, based on a distorted view of reality without there being in an intolerable situation, and heteroinduced, seen in defeated or colonized populations escaping their terrible reality. These authors show how there was mass suicide in Africa during colonization, and a suicide of about 400 people in the middle of the eighteenth century in British Guyana due to colonialism. Then there was Jonestown in Guyana in 1978 where 912 Americans killed themselves based on instructions from their paranoid leader Jim Jones (Lasaga, 1980). Over 200 children were killed by their parents. They had practiced self-poisoning many times before they actually took the real poison. Some believe that the suicides were involuntary because of the presence of armed guards (Stack, 1983). It may be that some were of this type. Jim Jones knew about and was influenced by mass martyrdom of the past (Robbins, 1989). The Japanese cult Friend of the Truth Church had a mass suicide in 1986 after their leader died (Takahashi, 1989). Some religious cults are violent (Bromley & Melton, 2002), and they typically have a hostile attitude toward the outside world (Mancinelli et al., 2002). There was a mass suicide of 39 members of Heaven's Gate religious cult in 1997. They believed that a spacecraft was coming for them. Chryssides (2011) called this a UFO religion. Members of a sect believe they have the truth, have restricted and then no contact with the outside world toward which they have a hostile attitude. The sect has a charismatic leader often suffering from a chronic delusion. The leader is commonly homosexual, volatile, and paranoid.

There are also suicide epidemics. In the 1970s and 1980s on the South Pacific Islands of Micronesia, there was a teenage suicide epidemic where the suicide rate was 10 times higher than in other places in the world, and the teenagers were killing themselves in the same way under the same circumstances (Gladwell, 2000). Arctic Indigenous youth have very high suicide rates, and Inuit youth have a rate 10 times that of Canada (Kral, 2012). Most hang themselves in their bedroom closet at night, usually facing the wall on the left side. They copy each other. Suicide existed in the Inuit past, but it was not the youth epidemic seen today that started in the mid-1980s. What was the tipping point that set off this trend? As Gladwell (2000, p. 24) wrote, "The tipping point is that magic moment when an idea, trend, or social behavior crosses a threshold, tips, and spreads like wildfire." Rather than finding how a trend actually starts, however, it is the process over time that is most interesting.

Mass homicide-suicide has also taken place (Lester, Stack, Schmidke, Schaller, & Muller, 2005). Marzuk Tardiff, and Hirsch (1992) found five types of homicide-suicides: spousal by enraged men, spousal due to declining health, depressed mothers killing their children, family where the male kills his whole family, and extrafamilial where typically a man kills innocent bystanders. The vast majority of perpetrators are male. In a study of 42 homicide-suicide cases in one American city by Harper and Voigt (2007), they found that 98% were done by handguns, 67% were intimate or domestic cases (spousal), alcohol and drugs played a small role, most were White, and 30% were Black. Culture seems to play a role because these murder-suicides are much more common in England and Wales than in the U.S. Stack (1997) found that the most common type of murder-suicide is the spousal one, or it could be killing a girlfriend. Usually the woman wants to leave the man or has just left him, and he is very jealous and controlling.

It is thus clear that social epidemics exist. Kahneman (2011, p. 217) writes that "people can maintain an unshakable faith in any proposition, however absurd, when they are sustained by a community of like-minded believers." Humans are highly suggestible (Schumaker, 1991). These epidemics are common in fads; take place among some mental disorders; and are seen in outbreaks in schools, work settings, and other localities. It is also seen in suicide. Mass suicides have moved from being exogenous or heteroinduced, caused by a terrible social environment, to endogenous or self-induced, resulting from a distorted view of reality. From slavery and colonialism to religious cults. We have suicide clusters, pacts, and murder-suicide, all related to contagion and copying others. There is a suicide epidemic among Arctic Indigenous youth, who are copying each other in both the reason for suicide and the method of suicide (Kral, in press). This would be a type of cluster suicide, although it has been going on for about 30 years. In earlier years, youth never killed themselves. So we need to understand the contagious side of suicide. This will be seen in Chapters 4 and 5.

4 Culture and Suicide

This section on anthropology is an appropriate next step to the history discussed in Chapter 2, cultural perspectives that I hope will demonstrate this needed conceptual direction for suicide studies. A cultural approach to suicide has been absent in the mainstream suicidology literature, and anthropological studies of suicide are rare (Colucci & Lester, 2013). The few newer books on culture and suicide will be reviewed here. The book *Essential Papers on Suicide* (Maltsberger & Goldblatt, 1996) does not include one about culture. A search using the keyword suicide in the Human Relations Area Files at Yale, however, produces 1,593 uses across 506 documents, and someone has yet to review suicide in this massive anthropological database. In this chapter I briefly review suicide from an anthropological point of view.

Providing an anthropological view of suicide in Perlin's *Handbook for the Study of Suicide*, Jean La Fontaine (1975) noted the importance of examining cultural values, indicating that anthropology's focus has been on social values and structure related to the incidence of suicide. La Fontaine identifies the effects of social forces on the individual as anthropology's domain, foregrounded against significant knowledge of the societies in question. His review of the research found support for Durkheim's theory of integration. His structuralist review, however, just preceded the interpretive turning point in the social sciences and anthropology.

Farberow (1975) edited an early book on culture and suicide. In it suicide is described for Native Americans, Argentina, Norway, Finland, Sweden, Britain, the Netherlands, Italy, Bulgaria, India, Israel, Taiwan, and Japan. Some cultures honored suicide while others condemned it. One sees that suicide differs depending on the country with regard to rates and methods. Cultural attitudes toward suicide differ. Suicidal ethnic differences in the U.S. are evident. Different Native American tribes had different patterns of suicide, while marital and family issues were important for suicide in India. The lower suicide rate in Norway was attributed to the interdependence of the people.

Two books have been published on ethnic differences in suicide in the U.S. (Leach, 2006; Leong & Leach, 2008). Leach (2006) indicates that European Americans make up about 90% of suicides in the U.S. African American women have low suicide rates, and African American men have a lower rate that White males, although the rate is increasing for younger African American men. Suicide is poorly understood among Asian Americans, who comprise a little over 2% of the U.S. population. They are more reluctant to seek professional help. East Asian women have the highest female suicide rate among all ethnic groups. Hispanic Americans are the largest ethnic minority population in the U.S. Among Hispanic Americans, the greater the assimilation into mainstream society, the higher the suicide rate. Suicide is more common among their youth. Hispanics have a lower suicide rate than non-Hispanic Whites. Native Americans have the highest suicide rate of any ethnic group, up to 3 times the national rate. Suicide occurs mainly with their youth, and it is low among the elderly. Alcohol, unemployment, poverty, and racism are tied to their suicides. LGBT individuals are at higher risk for suicide, as are elderly White men. Similar findings are reported in Leong and Leach (2008). Their book also covers suicide prevention for U.S. ethnic minority populations. Walker, Townley, and Asiamah (2008) present a culturally relevant model for suicide prevention for these populations. They have three key domains that such prevention should cover: accurate assessment and treatment, assessing the impact of race-related stressors and acculturative vulnerability, and ethnocultural resilience. They argue that prevention should be tied to the sociocultural and the ethnic reality of clients. Leach and Leong (2008) note that very little theory exists on culture and suicide to guide research.

Broz and Münster (2016) have edited an anthropological book on suicide. This book covers South India, Greenland, Mexico, India, Palestine, and Sri Lanka. Many of the accounts of suicide are ethnographic, looking at meanings of suicide and lives lived, looking at cultural sense-making of suicide. Their book seeks to "decenter Western ontologies, avoid the pathologizing psy-discourse and interrogate positivist frameworks of suicidology" (Broz & Münster, 2016, p. 10). The book examines ethnographic accounts looking at suicide, and how suicide is viewed in everyday life. The authors call for an anthropological imagination in suicidology. They see suicide as an expression of individual choice and as a sign of pathologies of power and larger structures. They see agency as central to suicide, yet spell out the tension of agency between conscious intent and responsibility versus being a more passive patient, a victim.

Honkasalo and Tuominen (2014) have edited a book on culture and suicide, where they also avoid pathologizing the suicidal. They see agency in suicide, yet it is also very much influenced by culture. They also examine suicide as choice versus as determined by something like an illness. They ask how culture can determine individual choices and decisions, and see the need to examine the person in their cultural and social context. They ask whether there are suicidal cultures. They see suicide as a decision based on cultural narratives. The book covers topics such as phenomenology, Plato, Stoic perspectives, the Middle Ages, the female suicide bomber, and men.

Colucci and Lester (2013) have also edited a book on culture and suicide. Their book addresses the need to go beyond psychiatric thinking about suicide and a need to look at cultural meanings of suicide, including gendered meanings. They show how people in different countries differ in their personal experiences of suicidal behavior, in their attitudes toward suicide, and their recommendations for preventing suicide. They point out the conceptual, methodological, and political challenges to conducting research on culture and suicide. Colucci (2013) has a chapter comparing attitudes toward suicide from Italian, Indian, and Australian people. Many differences are seen according to country and sex, and also according to religion, social class, and past experiences with one's own suicidality or that of friends or family.

A special issue on the anthropology of suicide was published in the journal *Culture, Medicine, and Psychiatry* in 2012 (Staples & Widger, 2012a). Suicide was examined ethnographically in South India, Sri Lanka, Southern Mexico, Afghanistan, Palestine, Arctic Canada, South Africa, England, Singapore, and Japan. Staples and Widger (2012b) hope to raise interest in and awareness about suicide in anthropology and make an anthropological contribution to suicidology, seeing suicide from within, in the lives of people. They see suicide as a social act.

Early and World Views

A review of suicide among "primitive peoples" was provided by Steinmetz (1894) over a century ago. Surveying reports from around the world, he described 42 cases and accounted for the reasons attributed to the suicides by the anthropologists and others who wrote these stories. Steinmetz found offended pride to be the most common motive, together with love, sorrow, fear of slavery and captivity, depression due to disappointment, illness, and family quarrels. He noted that most of these reasons are similar to those found for suicide in Western societies and quarreled with Morselli's (1882) argument that suicide was more common among "civilized" people. None of the cases described had been accompanied by an ethnographic analysis, and systematic details of this method were not yet developed. However, a number of particularities concerning reasons and methods for suicide specific to the various cultures were mentioned, indicating that suicide was also a phenomenon in form and function shaped by the local culture.

Malinowski (1932) provided an early ethnographic analysis of several cases of suicide among the Trobriand people. One, a young man, throws himself from a palm tree (*lo'u*). The method, details of dress, speech, and wailing prior to the jump followed Trobriand custom, after public denouncement of this man's incestuous affair with a first cousin. Malinowski fits this suicide into Trobriand beliefs and institutions, including village organization, tensions related to clan membership, and local law concerning exogamy and its breach. The young man chose one of two options for such a breach, the other being a ritual of spells and rites that might have exonerated him. Malinowski did not discuss why suicide was selected in this case but reported death as having been the man's "only one means of escape" (p. 78). Choosing one of two common fatal forms of suicide, the other being poison from the gall-bladder of a globe-fish, would take place within an "underlying attitude [that] is somewhat complex, embracing a desire of self-punishment, revenge, re-habilitation, and sentimental grievance" (p. 95). A less lethal method by vegetable poison used for stunning fish, treated successfully by induced vomiting, was common for cases of "lovers' quarrels, matrimonial differences, and similar cases" (p. 94). "Thus suicide, like sorcery, is a means of keeping the natives to the strict observance of the law, a means of preventing people from extreme and unusual types of behavior" (p. 98).

Much of early-twentieth-century American anthropology concerned itself with Native American peoples. Voegelin (1937) reviewed cases of suicide among tribes of northeastern California and found patterns based on known, yet reluctantly told to outsiders, stories over time. The first was described as an "old and elaborately patterned form" of suicide by the Wintu, following gambling loss or a dispute with one's mate, where the person, usually a male, would leave to a place by water and stay for days, diving repeatedly to the bottom until eventually drowning, and the body never being found (Voegelin, 1937, p. 445). A second pattern was around romantic disappointment and jealousy, followed by hanging by women and drowning by men; a third type was for the same reason but the method of death was by eating wild parsnip root. Wyman and Thorne (1945) described suicide among the Navaho, and through a set of key informants found it to have been rare but related primarily first to romantic jealously and quarreling or grief after losing relatives, and secondly to avoidance of consequences for crime or illness.

Iroquois and Algonquian suicide over a 300-year period in the Great Lakes and eastern Woodlands region was described by Fenton (1941), who also reported several common patterns. Suicide was relatively infrequent, averaging about one every nine years save for a few suicide epidemics. Between 1635 and 1650 apparently 20,000 Hurons killed themselves secondary to a smallpox epidemic, religious conversion by Jesuits, and "torture and persecution" by the Albany Dutch (p. 122). Male suicide predominated except for the Saulteaux, where female suicides outnumbered those of men. Male suicides were younger warriors, gamblers, or drunks, whereas women were middle-aged and their suicides were related to their being deserted or mistreated by their men, as revenge out of jealousy and betrayal in romantic relationships or to escape marriage. Suicide following a spouse's death was not uncommon among the Iroquois, and Fenton attributes this to Iroquois love and respect for their dead. Martydom was known in warfare and captivity, yet Iroquois, Algonquins, and Sioux were also known to have killed themselves to avoid capture. Suicide among the ill during smallpox epidemics was also reported among the Algonquin, Ojibwa, Saulteaux, and Pottawatomi. Suicide and attempted suicide were known to take place among native children in missionary residential schools under conditions of abuse and unhappiness (Milloy & McCallum, 1999). Summarizing the reported reasons for suicide among native groups, Fenton (1941) indicates their order of frequency as loss of status, avoidance of physical suffering, and jealousy/unfaithfulness in romantic relationships. He notes that Iroquois consistently stated that love was the only legitimate reason for suicide, yet argues that pre-Christian attitudes toward suicide among them would be very difficult to ascertain. Romantic problems have long been associated with suicide. Among Inuit many years ago, suicide was seen among the elderly who may be ill, during times of famine/poor hunting. Some would ask their children to kill them (Diamond, 2012; Laugrand & Oosten, 2010; Nourse, 1879; Rasmussen, 1929; Wallace, 1926). While the attitude toward suicide may have been ambivalent, Fenton points out that it became openly hostile with the coming of Christianity. As with other native traditions, however, Fenton indicated that there was a remarkable consistency in suicide motives and methods over a long period of time. Barbagli (2015) indicates that hunter-gatherer societies had altruistic suicide but also suicide for the same reasons as in the West, including disappointment in love, jealously, illness, unbearable pain, and loss of a loved one. Some suicides were to punish an offender or as revenge.

In more recent colonial times, suicide among Native North Americans has been extremely high in some communities. Those at highest risk have been primarily males between the ages of 15 and 24. While elderly White males are at a high demographic risk for suicide in mainstream North American society, suicide is still rare among native elders; it is strong tradition that elders are held at the highest level of respect in native society. If this tradition changes, I suspect that suicide among native elders will begin to climb. Berlin (1987) found that among Native Americans in the U.S. Southwest, those with the highest suicide rates were the least connected to their traditional cultural values. A more complex analysis of Native American suicide by Bachman and Strauss (1992) found that culture conflict, which he defined as a community holding onto traditional values while experiencing Westernization and social change, was associated with higher suicide rates. This pattern, together with poverty and unemployment, was found among the native communities with the higher rates of suicide. A similar pattern was found for Inuit in Greenland by Bjerregaard and Curtis (2002), who found that Inuit having both traditional and Western lifestyles had higher suicide rates than those holding more strongly to one or the other. Inuit in Greenland, Nunavut, and the northwest coast of Alaska have an extremely high rate of suicide among their youth. Kral (2012, 2013) found that family and sexual relationships have changed dramatically for Inuit since Canadian government colonization in the 1960s, leaving many youth feeling alone and rejected. Problems in these relationships were the primary reasons Inuit gave for suicide. Chandler and Lalonde (1998) found that suicide among First Nations in British Columbia was strongly and positively related to communities not having control over their social, educational, health, traditional, and other local institutions and practices. These authors interpreted this as a problem of cultural continuity, which I would interpret as a problem of community control over resources or collective agency. It is important to note here that recent reviews from a cultural perspective have indicated that suicide among native North Americans must be understood within the context of community powerlessness; identity diffusion; genocide; and rapid social, cultural, and economic change (Berlin, 1987; Echo-Hawk, 1997; Kirmayer, 1994; Kirmayer, Fletcher, & Boothroyd, 1998; May et al., 2002; Sinclair, 1998). Support has generally been found for Durkheim's theory of social integration/regulation for this population, and the theoretical model for suicide in the literature on native suicide has generally focused on the subculture of violence where suicide and other violent behaviors are seen as culturally learned and acceptable responses.

Jeffreys (1952) claims that one study found a "Samsonic" type of suicide as revenge in Africa, with the ghost going after a living person. Most studies of African suicide have supported Durkheim in terms of poor social integration among those killing themselves. Suicides were interpreted by the people in those societies as irrational and not entirely voluntary. Hanging was the most common method. Suicide contagion "expressed in supernatural terms" was also found to be common in East African societies. The effects of rapid Westernization/colonialism varied in that region, with a greater number of suicides when integration was lowered and fewer when social stability increased.

Studies of suicide in Asia have typically found patterns dissimilar to those in North America and Europe. In the early 1980s, suicide was generally found to decline with age after about 35 except for Japan, where suicide was U-shaped and higher among younger and older adults. Older adult suicide in Japan has been attributed to attitudes toward the elderly in that country becoming more negative, with elders playing a less important role in the nuclear family. Japanese suicidal elderly now commonly believe that they are a burden to their family (Takahashi, 1997), which has also been found among depressed and suicidal elderly in North America in the context of attitudes of "useless-ism" toward the elderly

(Richman, 1991, p. 155). Suicide among the elderly has more recently increased among the elderly in Asia, likely in accord with a decrease in respect for this segment of the population.

More recently, there has been a focus on suicide in China. Suicide is more frequent among women, whereas in most of the world men's rates are much higher than those of women. The lowest gender ratio for suicide in the world is found in China (Yip, 2001), and Asian Americans have small sex differences in the incidence of suicide compared with other ethnic groups in the U.S. The great majority of suicides in China occur in rural areas (93%), with the most common method being one of two popular pesticides or rat poison. Young rural women are the demographic group with the highest suicide rate. Like what is found in most countries in modern times, the elderly have high rates in China, however it is 5 times higher in rural versus urban areas (Phillips, Li, & Zhang, 2002). Although suicide data are unreliable in China prior to 1987, Phillips and his colleagues report that the suicide rates are likely related to rural modernization. Others speculate that the high female suicide rates are due to the low status of women (Diekstra, 1996, their lower education and higher illiteracy (Yip, 2001), or poverty and marital difficulties. Others attribute the young rural female suicides to the strict enforcement of birth quotas and common pressure into abortion or giving up of infants which, in rural China, is contrary to the emphasis there on children and their contribution to family labor (Reardon, 2002). Research looking at Chinese female suicide and pregnancy, abortion, sterilization, and fines for exceeding birth quotas, however, does not support this as the most significant factor although it was present in 16% of recent cases. Another study found that mental illness (notably depression) is lower among Chinese suicides, with 63% of suicides so attributed versus over 90% found in many studies elsewhere (Phillips, Yang, Zhang, Wang, Ji, & Zhou, 2002). Depression in the West has a much higher rate of suicidality, and in China there is much less guilt, despair, self-denigration, depressed mood, and suicidal ideation (Marsella, Sartorius, Jablensky, & Fenton, 1985; Schieffelin, 1985). Depression is very different across cultures (Good & Kleinman, 1985). It should be noted that expressions of distress tend toward somatization in China rather than emotional expression, as they do more often in North America and Europe, so one would need to examine the method used to obtain such data. Some similar risk factors to Western suicide were found for Chinese suicide, including depression, prior suicide attempts, negative life events (in this case primarily economic problems or serious illness or injury, although the most common immediately precipitating factor was a marital dispute), and being close to others with histories of suicidal behavior.

María Cátedra (1992) has written an ethnographic account of suicide among the Vaquieros of northwestern Spain. Suicide has been common among these people for some time, a group she describes as having a highly coherent cosmology that has remained relatively stable for generations. She situated suicide within the Vaquiero concept of death and illness, where illness is strongly associated with death, and death is a midpoint between Vaquiero concepts of life and the afterlife. Suicide is meaningful as part of the general loss of *gracia*, or grace, "the pleasure, fun, or interest in living" (p. 138). Loss of *gracia* means that Vaquieros, "although physically alive, are socially and cognitively dead" (p. 351). Those killing themselves were typically without *gracia* due to a loss or significant worsening of their role within the social network. Young women have a high suicide rate, and women lose considerable status and *gracia* after marriage. Being elderly and ill produces the same loss and suicide risk. While dedicated to an emic perspective, Cátedra noted that stories to strangers did not always match what was "really going on." In their stories to her, Vaquieros attributed mental illness ("suffering from nerves") to a great many more suicides than she believed was warranted, for example, similar to the findings of the only other study of suicide among these people 30 years earlier. Cátedra placed suicide within Vaquiero institutionalized unhappiness, as suggested in her closing words to her book: "An analysis of suicide should make clear cultural perceptions about when it is worth the trouble to live and when it is worth the trouble to die" (p. 355). Suicide is interpreted as one of a number of culturally constituted behaviors in response to an unhappy life in which one becomes disconnected from regular activity and/or socially disregarded, on the margins. Yet suicide is integrated within the local conception of death, with practices surrounding death highly integrated into Vaquiero life.

Anthropology

The literature on suicide and culture has mainly been cross-cultural or comparative, primarily using quantitative data. For a comparative picture of suicide this is essential information. Inferences about causality and about the experiences of suicidal individuals across cultures remain, however, inferences based on theory and on often well-informed hunches based on nomothetic data. There is little cultural research on suicide that is "deeper" and "thicker," on which inferences and theory are derived up from the experiences of the people being studied. Why do young, rural, Chinese women take their lives in such large numbers? Why is there a suicide epidemic among young Inuit? What are the experiences of First Nations youth in BC communities where community control of essential and cultural services and activities is high, such that suicide is viewed as a less likely option when one is otherwise distressed? There is a paucity of, and significant need for, the ethnographic study of suicide to be able to address these kinds of questions. Yet there is a new look at the anthropology of suicide, and there has been a call for qualitative research on suicide (Hjelmeland & Knizek, 2010).

Farberow (1975) indicated the importance of knowing about how differences in attitudes toward suicide across cultures influence suicidal behaviors. There is recent evidence that more accepting attitudes toward suicide as an option are highly correlated with suicide rates across 35 countries (Stack & Kposowa, 2008). Again, these data are telling, but needed are ethnographies such as Cátedra's with the Vaquieros that will permit a closer understanding of such attitudes within cultural and personal systems of meaning. Counts (1991) described suicide among the Maring of Papua New Guinea, where only women would take their lives. She outlines the cultural model and rules for suicide, including collective and personal circumstances leading to the choice of suicide and its particular method. Counts argues that suicide prevention will be impossible, for example, without knowing this cultural patterning. Lutz (1988) has similarly shown how suicide is culturally scripted by the Ifaluk people in Micronesia, sequenced through a particular action (e.g., moral condemnation of another), followed by an emotion (e.g., justifiable anger), which can then lead to suicide, followed by several weeks of sightings of the malicious spirit of the deceased. An anthropological view aims to show how suicide is a part of the life and death of a community, how it is understood by its members.

Firth (1961) described scripted suicide methods for Indigenous people of Tikopia, an island of Western Polynesia in the southwestern Pacific. The middle-aged and elderly hanged themselves with a thin cord or fishline by tying the end to a beam in a house and running with force, dying rather quickly. Women, especially younger ones, swam out to sea, while younger men paddled their canoes out to sea. These latter forms of death were interpreted by the people as "splendid" (123), which the spirits would not oppose, yet they would object if men hanged themselves. A common rationale for young people making suicide attempts was to be reprimanded by one's parents, boys by their fathers in particular. Firth (129) described these as "expected norms" that in turn function "to mitigate parental discipline" by making parents afraid of causing such behavior.

In India there was *sati*, suicide by widows after their husbands died. The widow would be burnt in a fire. The ritual began with a declaration of the widow's intent. There were processions, feasts, banquets, dances, songs, and the participation of sometimes thousands of people. The widow would wear her bridal gown, wedding jewelry, and cover her head with bridal flowers. In 1987 an 18-year-old did this after eight months of marriage when her husband died, and there were 4,000 onlookers (Barbagli, 2015). It was an act of free will. This was a suicide that was praised. It began after the third century CE. *Sati* made the widow "a supernatural being, endowed with enormous powers, and she would bring prestige for many years to their descendants on both sides of the family" (Barbagli, 2015, p. 211). Widows also killed themselves in China after about 1300, however unlike *sati* they killed themselves in solitude.

Ellen Corin provides insight into how suicide can be seen from what she calls an anthropological imagination. Pointing out that inferences about culture cannot be made easily from cross-national suicide data, Corin argues that, from an anthropological perspective, culture is embedded in all aspects of life and must be examined in this manner. She advises that suicidal "discourse and behavior have to be resituated in the context of the person's life frame and of his or her position within a collective frame" (p. 216). Life and collective frames hold metonymic relationships at many levels. Interviews with persons of particular groups identified at high and low risk could explore meanings within these frames. A discrepancy between expectations and realities in the context of social change has been one common finding across studies of suicide, yet suicide as an option is as culturally scripted as are other choices. Corin suggests that an ethnographic approach to suicide might be studied across three dimensions:

> The sense of future, the perceived relationship between self and the world, and a feeling of personal value. These three themes could provide a way to systematize the study of how large-scale transformations, sociopolitical conditions, and the cultural changes associated with modernity and postmodernity affect the lives of . . . people in particular groups or subgroups particularly at risk for . . . suicide.
>
> (p. 218)

The writing on suicide by Paperno, Cátedra, Counts, and Corin cited above constitutes a cultural anthropological framework that has been otherwise missing in suicidology. A number of scholars have more recently argued that theory in suicidology is largely absent, and the common cliché that suicide is "multidimensional" perpetuates a closed, and in my opinion tail-chasing, approach to the study and understanding of suicide. Suicide is certainly multidimensional, but not all the dimensions have been explored (White et al., 2016). We will now look at how culture is internalized, how suicide can be internalized, and how culture can provide motives for action.

Internalization

The study of cultural transmission is multidisciplinary. Internalization is a core concept in cultural psychology and anthropology (D'Andrade, 1995; Hutchins, 1996; Stigler, Shweder, & Herdt, 1990; Zittoun & Gillespie, 2015). It can also be called bidirectional cultural transfer, the active construction of cultural messages in the mind. Strauss (1992, p. 1) asks the important question, "How do cultural messages get under people's skin?" Schafer (1968, p. 8) has internalization as "a portion of the external world . . . becomes an integral part of the internal world."

Social norms are internalized and transmitted across generations. Cultural models and schemas are internalized. A schema "is an interpretation which is frequent, well organized, memorable, which can be made from minimal cues, contains one or more prototypic instantiations, is resistant to change, etc." (D'Andrade, 1992a). Similarly, a cultural model "refers to shared, recognized, and transmitted internal representations" (D'Andrade, 1992b, p. 230). As Geertz (1973, p 83) wrote, "Human thinking is primarily an overt act conducted in terms of the objective materials of the common culture, and only secondarily a private matter." Spiro (1997) describes three theories of cultural internalization. Classical Marxist theory has the social system serving the interests of the ruling class, while most people are in the "exploited" classes who are not interested in the social system but their internalization is a "false consciousness." Classical socialization theory has children socialized and socially conditioned, which produced internalization. Then the theory of cultural determinism believes that culture forms all cognitions, motivations, and emotions, and culture constitutes the person, making internalization by transmission required.

The concept of internalization was developed by G. H. Mead, L. S. Vygotsky, and James Mark Baldwin. Vygotsky saw internalization as "a process involved in the transformation of social phenomena into psychological phenomena" (Wertsch, 1985, p. 63). It is a "distinguishing feature of human psychology" (Vygotsky, 1978, p. 58). Consciousness was, for Vygotsky, social. Stemming from Vygotsky and others is a situated cognition movement since the 1980s, where cognition is socially located (Bechtel, 2009). As Leont'ev (1981) wrote, "The process of internalization is not the *transferal* of an external activity to a preexisting internal 'plane of consciousness': it is the process in which this internal plane is *formed*." Throop (2003, p. 111) defines internalization as a person's "ability to become personally (cognitively, emotionally, and motivationally) invested in [cultural] knowledge," and in his review of theories of internalization, negative emotional ideas are also internalized. Collins, Gleason, and Semsa (1997, p. 139) have internalization as "the processes by which individuals acquire beliefs, attitudes, or behavioral regulations from external sources and progressively transform those external regulations into personal attributes, values, or regulatory styles." It may be a form of enculturation or socialization. Bar-Tal (2000) describes the process through which societal beliefs are transmitted. People have to be exposed to the contents of the belief, it has to be comprehended, it has to be perceived as valid, it has to be relevant, and it has to fulfill certain needs. The idea of suicide would fit into this scheme. Similarly, Schönpflug (2009b) argues that true imitation can only occur if the imitator understands the goals and intentions of the model. The message also has to be accepted. This would be the case for suicide.

Various types of internalization have been studied, including doing schoolwork, performing chores around the house, attending religious functions, health, and materialism (Grolnick, Deci, & Ryan, 1997). We copy groups as well as individuals. Spiro (1987) developed five levels of internalization. In the first level, a person becomes acquainted with part of a cultural system. Level two is the person understanding cultural meanings. Internalization takes place at level three, where the person is engaged in the cultural system that influences her or his behavior, and holds cultural meanings to be true, correct, or right. The cultural model becomes a personal belief system. In level four, the cultural system is highly salient and held with conviction. It is in the person's mind and emotions. At level five, culturally constituted beliefs instigate motivation and action. LeVine (1973) had three modes of cultural adoption: willing conformity, where there is a match between human needs and social norms; coerced conformity, where there is pressure from social norms to conform; and normative pluralism, where people match norms and values to their personalities.

Internalization is relational, an interdependence between self and others. Lawrence and Valsiner (1993, pp. 152–153) identified internalization as "the transformation of culturally provided input into the person's active process of co-construction of the self . . . the coordinating and recombining previously existing knowledge structures," a restructuring of new and old. It is as Bruner (1990, p. 12) notes, impossible to construct a human psychology on the basis of the individual alone. Social structure creates internalized meanings about one's own behavior (Stets & Burke, 2003). Social norms affect intrinsic predispositions (Etzioni, 2000). Spiro (1997) also notes that consummatory propositions are internalized, ones that meet a person's needs or desires. There is a motivation, possibly also inspired by culture, to internalize particular ideas. Deci, Eghrari, Patrick, and Leone (1994) identify two types of internalization: introjection, where the person takes in information but does not identify with it or own it; and integration, where information is assimilated with one's sense of self, one accepts responsibility for one's behavior related to this information from culture, and the person is self-determined, volitional. This self-determination or agency is in keeping with what other writers argue, and with Tarde, that there is no tabula rasa mind but people are agentic (Grolnick et al., 1997; Mattingly, Lutkehaus, & Throop, 2008; Spiro, 1997). Latour (2002) argues that for Tarde, the link between agency and imitation/influence was essential. As Candea (2010, p. 3) wrote, it is for Tarde "the indissociability of acting and being acted upon." In a study, Deci et al. (1994) found that self-determination actually promotes integrative internalization. One's needs are met through internalization. One chooses, both consciously and unconsciously, what one will accept privately. Tarde (1903) believed that social or contagious imitation could be conscious or unconscious.

Cultural models or schemas can have directive or motivational force. Internalized meanings and values can have motivational power (Chirkov, Ryan, & Willness, 2005). Schemas can instigate action; they can be motivating and can function as goals (D'Andrade, 1992a). Schemas can be internalized and take the form of goals that have motivational force (Morling & Kitayama, 2008). Goals can be contagious as inferred from other individuals' actions (Aarts, Dijksterhuis, & Dik, 2008). Even scripts can generate goals (Schank & Abelson, 1977). Suicide is a cultural script, as the motives and methods of suicide are particular to local places and people. The method of suicide varies considerably across cultures and countries, and is the same within those cultures and countries (Ajdacic et al., 2008). The motivations for suicide are also cultural. For example, suicide among British farmers is mostly due to their perceptions of family problems, but farmers in India report reasons being indebtedness and monetary concerns (Behere & Bhise, 2009). Domestic problems was the most common reason for suicide in Pakistan (Khan, 1998), interpersonal problems in Mexico (Chavez-Hernandez, Paramo, Leenaars, & Leenaars, 2006), and breaking up with a girlfriend for Inuit male youth in Arctic Canada (Kral, 2012).

If suicide is a cultural idea from motivation to method, how do some individuals take it on as personal script while others ignore it (see Throop, 2003; Toomela, 1996)? The terms culture and internalization are used in biology, and internalization may be too simple a concept for the confluence of mind and culture. It implies a unidirectional movement of something, in this case a thing called culture into a thing called psyche or mind. The questions "why" and "how" are the challenging ones here, and need to capture both the individual mind and collective, popular norms. Throop (2003) shows how the person internalizing cultural models is active and agentic, that emotion and motivation are included, and together with Toomela (1996) shows how internalization is both verbal and non-verbal, personally meaningful, and not always completely conscious. Lawrence and Valsiner (1993) add that the psychoanalytic concept of identification is important in internalization, and write that imitation is "the driving force of developmental change" (p. 161). Thus a person who is already very distressed and even suicidal can internalize the idea of suicide as a personal choice, which includes reasons for doing it and how to do it. An Inuit youth knows relatives and friends who have killed themselves, a very personal resonance, knows that suicide has become common among other youth and can identify with them, and may even have the horrific image of a hanging relative found in the closet. This can become a cultural model of suicide as choice, with culturally common reasons and methods for suicide. Regarding suicide, why do some individuals accept the idea into their personal range of choices, and how do popular norms become such?

Culture and mind will meet when they are in synch, when there is an individual openness to particular cultural messages. These are the "semiotic connectives" between elements within a cultural system and these elements with individual personalities.

The Idea of Suicide

In two previous publications I developed a theoretical approach to suicide from a cultural angle, seeing suicide as a contagious phenomenon (Kral, 1994, 1998). Lester (2008) has noted that no cultural theory of suicide exists. I expanded Edwin Shneidman's (1971, 1985) earlier theory of suicide, where he saw suicide as a function of the necessary and sufficient ingredients of perturbation and lethality. Perturbation is exactly that: stress, anguish, pain, depression, pressure, shame, agony, most mental disorders, and so on. Shneidman's definition of lethality varied, however, from personality characteristics to the lethality of the method chosen. Guns are more lethal than pills. I redefined lethality as *the idea of death*, in this case of suicide. Alfred North Whitehead (1933, p. 53) wrote that an idea "has a creative power, making possible its own approach to realization." Suicide is a conscious, volitional idea, usually planned and perhaps even practiced. Lethality is a cognitive construct. Perturbation does not cause suicide. It does cause the person to do something about the perturbation. This is the function of perturbation. One decides what to do about it, and this decision may be adaptive or maladaptive. I see suicide as a function of perturbation and cognitive lethality. Shneidman's (1993, 1995) most recent theory of suicide was without the lethality and was only about perturbation, which he called "psychache." He believed that psychache or perturbation alone causes suicide. I disagree, as perturbation only causes a person to try to do something about it. What one does is open. Why, for some, is suicide seen as the only reasonable alternative? Again, the idea of suicide is internalized and becomes a personal belief system, is highly salient, and is held with conviction and personal investment (Spiro, 1987; Throop, 2003). As Spiro (1984) wrote, "Many of our thoughts and emotions are (what might be termed) 'culturally constituted'." Rosaldo (1984, p. 140) noted that "cultural patterns—social facts—provide a template for all human action, growth, and understanding."

I am not arguing for a sociocultural determinism, where private thoughts are replicas of public messages. Two people will not be affected by culture in the same way. People have different reasons for engaging in cultural models; they are agentic and can make choices. Some are more open to particular cultural messages. In the case of suicide, some people are more vulnerable to the idea. This will be when they have very negative thoughts about themselves, possibly hating themselves, even wishing they were dead. Depression can do this. People have agency, even with the idea of suicide. We may be molded by our culture, but we do so with our own free will. The human is no blank slate being molded by external forces like culture (Pinker, 2002). As Sugarman and Martin (2010, p. 162) point out, "Human agency is both determined and self-determining." Most people will not internalize suicide as something highly salient. Yet some will choose this as an option to end their perturbation. We are aware of many suicide risk factors that will make such a choice easier.

My model or theory of suicide fits with the theory of Gabriel Tarde, whose theory of culture was that people imitate each other, and with the many people who have written about internalization. Tarde will be discussed in detail in the next chapter. According to Vygotsky, we internalize almost everything. We are cultural beings, shaped by the people we grow up with. Is it possible that the idea of suicide will be generated spontaneously in a person's mind when they are perturbed without external influence other than stress? This is how suicide is generally understood. It is what I have called the origin myth in suicidology, seeing suicide as coming from an individual (Kral, 1998). If most of our ideas and goals are internalized from culture, there is no reason to believe that suicide is not so internalized. The mind is social. Jenkins (1994, p. 111) shows that there is a "cultural specificity to 'sadness' and 'suffering.'" Looking at how illness and disease concepts vary across cultures, Valsiner and van der Veer (2000, p. 42) report that "patients feel miserable but how this feeling is conceptualized and expressed depends upon the available cultural disease models." This is referred to as an idiom of distress, a cultural idiom, where the experience and expression of distress and illness are culturally driven (Nichter, 1981, 2010). Suicide is a cultural schema, particular to specific cultures. Keller (1992, p. 59) indicates that schemas account for order, inference, and directive force; they are "culturally derived, knowledge-generated structures which facilitate comprehension and inferencing." She adds that schemas can also be called mental models, folk theories, and metaphors. The schema for suicide will include the popular methods of and reasons for suicide. This is internalized and, for some, acted out. Gergen (2010) has noted that the turn from the Enlightenment view of the person from the eighteenth century, looking at reason, science, and the Cartesian dualistic view of mind and body, to the person being seen as a product of the social and cultural context, is a major historical transformation in how we see the person. My approach to suicide thus sees suicide as an idea that is internalized through culture by vulnerable people.

In addition to cultural idioms of distress, there are cultural psychiatric syndromes. The *Diagnostic and Statistical Manual of Mental Disorders* used to contain a section on cultural syndromes, but now it is called "Glossary of Cultural Concepts of Distress" (APA, 2013). Nine are listed, and they include Kufungisisa among the Shoa of Zimbabwe, anxiety, panic depression, and irritability caused by thinking too much. There is Susto among Latinos in Mexico and Central and South America, attributed to a frightening event that causes the soul to leave the body resulting in unhappiness and sickness. The concept of cultural syndrome in psychiatry was founded in 1951 by Yap, who critiqued psychiatric universalism. One cultural syndrome was Koro among the Malays and Southern Chinese, where a man believes that his penis is receding into his abdomen and thinks he will die. The man panics and may be taken to the hospital. Roy, Hazarika, Bhattacharya, Nath, and Saddichha (2011) found that after a few men reported having Koro, there was a statewide epidemic of this disorder affecting thousands of men. They thought that mobile phones helped spread this epidemic.

Yap (2018/1951) wrote about such "hysterical contagions" and found that, as in Chapter 3, they have always existed. He saw psychiatry as a Western way of looking at the world and supported a relativistic view (Crozier, 2018). Yet some psychiatric syndromes are culture-bound to America, for example eating disorders, which have now spread to other parts of the world. Schizophrenia has better symptomatic and social outcomes in "developing," less industrialized societies. These outcomes are quite favorable for a large number of these patients (Hopper & Wanderling, 2000; Hopper, Harrison, & Wanderling, 2007). It is not clear why these differences exist in schizophrenia, and good ethnographic research is needed to explore this. It is clear that culture has a huge influence on psychiatric symptoms and disorders, and "cultural concepts of distress" should apply all around the world.

Closing the Exits

In 1989 Clarke and Lester (1989) published a book called *Suicide: Closing the Exits*. In this book they show how suicide method is scripted, and when the popular method of suicide is removed, people do not tend to seek another method, what is called displacement. No displacement was found for gun suicide after the 1977 amendments to the Canadian federal gun control law (Carrington & Moyer, 1994), nor after a barrier was installed on a river bridge in Brisbane, Australia (Law, Sveticic, & De Leo, 2014). Gun control did reduce suicides in Canada (Leenaars, Moksony, Lester, & Wenckstern, 2010). The Canadian Firearms Act of 1992 reduced suicides in Quebec (Caron, 2010). The script is broken once the method is removed. This happened in England and Wales, where oven gas was detoxified. In 1960, domestic gas accounted for about half of all suicides, but by 1980 gas was used in only 0.2% of suicides. The suicide rate in the U.S. increased due to the availability of handguns (Clarke & Lester, 1989; Wiebe, 2003). The rate of handgun suicide increased by more than 50% between 1959 and 1984. States with stricter handgun control laws had lower rates of suicide by guns. Gun ownership is associated with suicide (Cummings, Koepsell, Grossman, Savarino, & Thompson, 2011; Kellerman et al., 1992; Killias, 1993; Kposowa, 2013; Lester, 1988; Miller, Lippmann, Azrael, & Hemenway, 2007; Miller, Azrael, & Hemenway,

2002), and also with homicide (Siegel, Ross, & King, 2013). Thus, owning a handgun increases suicide risk (Anestis & Houtsma, 2018). Gun ownership is associated with living in a social gun culture, where having a gun is acceptable (Kalesan, Villarreal, Keyes, & Galea, 2016). Gun ownership is also associated with individualism (Celinska, 2007). Firearm availability increases suicide risk for up to six years following the purchase (Brent & Bridge, 2003). The association between gun availability and suicide has been found around the world (Bangalore & Messerli, 2013). It has been found that gun control legislation reduces suicide rates (Anestis et al., 2015; Lambert & Silva, 1998; Lubin et al. 2010; Rodriguez Andres & Hempstead, 2011; Sloan et al., 1990).

Suicide Hotspots

Suicide "hotspots" are places where many people kill themselves. Suicide hotspots are specific sites, usually in a public location, are frequent places for suicide, have easy access, and gain a reputation and media attention as a place for suicide. Mount Mihara in Japan became a "suicide shrine" in the 1930s. Two students jumped into its crater, and then tourists began to arrive in large numbers, where a suicide could be seen almost every day. Most suicide jumpers do it from high-rise residential housing units, and media reports encourage imitation (Beautrais, 2007). The famous hotspot in the U.S. is the Golden Gate Bridge. Suicides began only weeks after the Golden Gate Bridge was opened in 1937, and they have continued. Given its height of 220 feet over the water, death from jumping is almost inevitable. There were 39 suicides in 2016 and 33 in 2017, more than one every two weeks. Bateson (2012) describes one study that surveyed almost 3,000 adults across the U.S. asking them if they thought a suicide barrier on the Golden Gate Bridge would save lives. Over two-thirds of respondents believed that most jumpers would kill themselves another way.

Stack, Bowman, and Niederkrotenhaler (2018) found 33 sites in the world that are suicide hotspots, including several in Japan. They report on suicides at Mt. Fuji in Japan, where many people kill themselves. The last year suicides were reported was 2003, and there were 105 suicides. Most are male between 21 and 50 years of age, and most suicides are by hanging. Most suicides do not carry any personal identification. Takahashi (1988) interviewed suicide attempters from this location and found that they felt Mt. Fuji was a sanctuary where suicide was allowed and believed they would receive much sympathy for their act. They wanted to belong to the group of people who had killed themselves there before. This is what Niezen (2009) found for suicidal Indigenous youth in Canada, that they felt like they belonged with other youth who had killed themselves. Takahashi found a correlation between media coverage of suicides at Mt. Fuji and the suicides there. Mt Fuji is known as the most spiritual place in Japan. There is also the black forest called Aokigahara in Japan where many people hang themselves. It is a thick forest of 12 square miles. Six people are assigned to suicide prevention patrol in the black forest every day of the year.

The city of Bern has a high number of suicides by jumping. The highest number of suicides took place at the city's Muenster Terrace, their hotspot. A safety net was installed in 1998 and no suicides took place at that location after this. Suicides decreased in Bern, so there was no evidence for displacement or substitution to other jumping areas. There is evidence that barriers and safety nets on bridges where suicide has been popular significantly decrease or stop such suicides (Pirkis et al., 2013). There have been railway suicide clusters in Australia, where people copied each other in this method of suicide (Too, Pirkis, Milner, Bugeja, & Spittal, 2017). An epidemic of charcoal-burning suicide has taken place in Taiwan, and media coverage encouraged imitation (Chang, Gunnell, Wheeler, Yip, & Sterne, 2010). Media also influenced this method of suicide in South Korea (Huh et al., 2009).

5 Cultural Mimesis in Suicide
A Return to Diffusion and Gabriel Tarde

Suicide is a performative act. In the book *Suicide as a Dramatic Performance*, Martinez (2015) sees suicide as symbolic action directed toward a real or imagined audience, and as an act of expressive communication. It is a social phenomenon, learned from others in a cultural context, identified with similar others, and performed for an audience. In this chapter I will show how Tarde's theory of culture as imitation can be applied to suicide. I show how suicide is contagious and that the idea of suicide is spread through the process of diffusion. I argue that diffusion theory in anthropology died a premature death and that it belongs to the newer look in anthropology on cultural transmission and the propagation of ideas. Suicide, according to Staples and Widger (2012a, pp. 186, 187), is "a problem that seems to go to the heart of human sociality . . . one that is an anthropological concern."

Diffusion is usually the spread of cultural traits from one society to the next. I believe diffusion can also spread within a society. Contagion can be conscious or unconscious. Strauss (1992, p. 12) refers to "cognitive patterns unconsciously extracted from repeated experience." Imitation implies conscious copying, but it does not have to be. For example, people will copy each other when yawning or laughing without thinking about doing so. Humans imitate each other more than any other animal (Bentley, Earls, & O'Brien. 2011) Suicide is a conscious act, but some of the ideas behind it may be outside of awareness. Diffusion is thus the spread of the idea of suicide, and vulnerable people may imitate it through contagion.

Contagion and Epidemics

Suicide is contagious. Phillips (1974) first showed that suicide reports in newspapers resulted in higher suicide rates in the paper's catchment area, which he called the "Werther effect" after Goethe's suicided hero Werther was apparently copied by men in Germany imitating his method and manner of dress. *The Sorrows of Young Werther* was banned in Germany in the late 1700s. It was not uncommon to find Werther's novel beside bodies after a suicide in early America, where the book was very popular (Bell, 2012). This media contagion of suicide has been replicated in studies and found to explain sudden increases in suicide (Gould, Jamieson, & Romer, 2003; Romer, Jamieson, & Jamieson, 2006). The media encourage more suicide attempts than suicides (Stack, 2002). The increase in suicide in the U.S. in the late eighteenth century had many newspapers writing stories about this epidemic, and a congressman warned printers that "the spirit of imitation is contagious," that such reporting could be dangerous (Bell, 2012, p. 35). There is now considerable evidence that suicide can be contagious. "Suicide rate up after coverage," read a headline in the Montreal *Gazette* (November 17, 2001). This media contagion effect is now well known, and news stories today rarely cover suicides. It is interesting that media contagion of social problems was also part of the discourse in France in the later 1800s (Valsiner & van der Veer, 2010).

The suicide-by-media effect has the largest effect on youth and then the elderly, mostly males (Stack, 2000c). The new suicides subsequent to these stories typically have characteristics similar to the suicides reported (Gould & Shaffer, 1986; Stack, 2000b). It is worth noting that Neal Miller and John Dollard (1941, p. 264), a psychologist and anthropologist writing about the psychology of diffusion over 60 years ago, made a similar observation: "The more nearly the copier and the model share their social habits, the more easy is the copying transaction." Suicide contagion research has focused almost exclusively on media reporting of suicide, and this literature has not been integrated with anthropological theory or research, nor with any theory of suicide.

It has been reported that the most influential models of media suicide contagion are entertainment or political celebrities (Booth, 2010; Lee, Hwang, & Stack, 2014; Stack, 1987, 2003). After Marilyn Monroe's suicide, for example, there was a 13% increase in suicide in the U.S., and in South Korea an almost 50% increase following a celebrity suicide (Abrutyn & Mueller, 2014a). As I write this, two celebrities recently killed themselves, designer Kate Spade and chef Anthony Bourdain. Kate Spade's sister said that Kate had been obsessed over Robin Williams's suicide. Williams hanged himself using a belt, while Spade used a scarf on a doorknob, as did the well-known designer L'Wren Scott, who hanged herself two years earlier. Imitation? The first newspaper ever printed in the U.S. featured a suicide story on its front page (Bell, 2012). As suicides were increasing in the nineteenth century, so were newspaper stories about the suicides. The concern over media contagion of suicide has prompted media guidelines for suicide reporting (Gould et al., 2003; Pirkis et al., 2006). A common anthropological perspective on suicide is that it follows "cultural scripts" and "idioms" and is "culturally constructed" (Widger, 2012; Staples & Widger, 2012; Counts, 1991). Canetto (2008) proposed a theory of cultural scripts of suicide. An important question is, if suicide is contagious via the media, can it be contagious in general? Norms are created within social networks (Hechter & Opp, 2001). What might all this tell us about suicide?

Berger (2013, p. 21) describes six principles of contagion, which he defines as "likely to spread. To diffuse from person to person via word of mouth and social influence." He derived these principles through analyzing hundreds of contagious messages, products, and ideas. They are (1) social currency, the sharing of stories and attitudes; (2) triggered, or the accessibility of information, stimuli in the environment, being triggered to think about something; (3) emotion, as positive emotions assist in people copying each other, however some negative emotions can do this if there is already a negative emotion in the receiver, and emotions can motivate people into action; (4) public, or the power of observability, information made public; (5) practical value, meaning the information is useful; and (6) stories, which are important for cultural learning, and this can be the story of someone's suicide, which we have seen via the media can be contagious. Walters (1968) reported that emotional arousal is correlated with people imitating each other. Schönpflug (2009a) also reports that cultural content including emotion will be more likely to be transmitted. Berger is interested in how things catch on, such as through attractive pricing, advertising, ease of use, effectiveness, being seen as more true, and being seen through influential people. He reports that word of mouth is behind 20–50% of all purchasing decisions.

René Girard developed a theory of mimesis (meaning imitation in Greek) since the 1960s, where human desire is imitative rather than being an expression of an autonomous self (Garrels, 2011a; Palaver, 2013). Human motivation is based on imitation, and it is mediated by culture, primarily through the unconscious. Mimetic desire creates a need based on a model's influence. Girard believes that we desire what others desire, with mimetic desire being the imitation of another's desire. His was a theory of culture very similar to Tarde's. Girard said, "It is clear that all human relations are based on imitation" (Garrels, 2011b, p. 216). He found that violence is one of the most imitative behaviors in humans. Suicide is a form of violence.

Durkheim and Tarde

The sociologist Durkheim (1951 [1897]) saw suicide as a problem of social integration and regulation. Breault (1994) found empirical support for Durkheim's theory, particularly egoistic suicide as a result of low integration. Joiner (2005) has shown how the lack of perceived belongingness is a suicide risk factor, as in egoistic suicide. Yet Kushner and Sterk (2005) show that social integration or capital does not necessarily lead to fewer suicides. Sociologists have also demonstrated that certain demographic factors such as marriage, ethnicity, social class, and religion are tied to suicide rates (Stack, 2000a, 2000b).

Durkheim's theory of suicide, low integration and regulation, can be seen as a theory of *perturbation*, not of suicide. People in these conditions are perturbed, upset, not necessarily suicidal. Why some may choose suicide as an answer to their perturbation is our question. The theorist who may aid in the understanding of this question, of the social nature of suicide, was Durkheim's rival, Gabriel Tarde. Durkheim wrote *Le Suicide* in part to spite Tarde (Besnard, 2002). Tarde (1903) influenced diffusionist theory in anthropology (see Kinnunen, 1996), as his theory of culture and society was that people imitate each other, that this is how ideas are spread. Valsiner and van der Veer (2000) believe that Tarde was a founder of sociology and social psychology. Niezen (2014) indicates that Tarde, unlike Durkheim, wanted a sociology based not on objectivity but on inter-subjectivity. Imitation for Tarde is founded on shared language "within a specific cultural framework" (Abrutyn & Mueller, 2014b, p. 703). Individuals evaluate and interpret whether they will conform. Tarde (1903, p. 367) wrote that "if a good idea is introduced . . . it propagates itself without any difficulty." Emotions, he argued, were mutually contagious, "*les sentiments . . . facilement contagieuse*" (feelings, states of mind are readily contagious) (Tarde, 1904, p. 295). He also wrote that imitation could be conscious or unconscious (Tarde, 1903). "To sum up, everything which is social and non-vital or non-physical in the phenomenon of societies is caused by imitation" (Tarde, 1903, p. 50). Imitation worked as a function of degree of or conviction in belief (*de conviction, de croyance*) and emotion (*de desire*) of model and recipient individuals and nations (Tarde, 1904, pp. 28, 37, 70). Tarde also attended to individual differences, and although he did not articulate it to any great extent he postulated strong relationships across personality, imitation, and culture (Clark, 1969). Winslow (1972, p. 108) wrote a book on suicide in 1840 where he had a chapter on imitative and epidemic suicide, writing about suicide contagion and that the human is an "imitative animal." Durkheim (1951 [1897]) devoted a chapter in his book *Le Suicide* to arguing against the role of imitation in suicide. Imitation was too psychological and intersubjective. Yet he wrote that "suicide is very contagious" and "perhaps no other phenomenon is more readily contagious" (pp. 96, 132). Tarde (1903, p. 25) wrote about "contagious imitation." Douglas (1967) noted that Durkheim's book on suicide contained many contradictory theoretical arguments, and Karsenti (2010) indicated that Durkheim was ambiguous about the role of imitation.

Abrutyn and Mueller (2014c) identify five laws from Tarde's writing, all laws of imitation, which are (1) logical, in which the person has agency and chooses and identifies with role models; (2) existing ideas will spread faster than new ones; (3) emotional where emotions are contagious (Hatfield & Cacioppo, 1993; Hess & Blairy, 2001) and people close to each other are more influenced by each other's emotions; (4) prestige where status yields influence; and (5) propinquity, which is one's similarity to others, proximity between people, identifying with models who are like the person. It has been found that people are more suicidal at a later time if family members or friends were suicidal. Studies have found that friends will imitate friends regarding suicidal behavior. People with no history of suicidality can become suicidal following exposure to a suicidal friend or family member (Mueller & Abrutyn, 2015; Mueller, Abrutyn, & Stockton, 2015). A friend's suicidal behavior is linked to a person's suicidality (Bearman & Moody, 2004; Rew, Thomas, Horner, Resnick, & Beuhring, 2001). A large study by Liu (2006) found that among adolescents, a friend's suicide attempt predicts the adolescent's own suicide attempt. Suicide and suicide attempters may induce serious suicidal thoughts in others (Baller & Richardson, 2009). Thus, exposure to suicidal people increases risk.

Role models evoke a shared identity with the role aspirant; they need to embody the role aspirants' already existing goals (the person is already suicidal), leading to motivation to work toward those goals, and are representations of the possible (Morgenroth, Ryan, & Peters, 2015). The notion of agency was important to Tarde, as he wrote, "Do we not move, by imperceptible degrees, from a considered volition to a more or less mechanical habit?" (cited in Candea, 2010, p. 3). One can say that, according to Tarde (1904), suicide has a social logic (Kral, 1994). Behavioral imitation is part of culture where people actively identify with a model or look up to that model (Kitayama & Uskul, 2011); imitative learning is a basic form of cultural learning. Dijkster-huis (2005, p. 208) argues that imitation "constitutes the 'social glue' that makes us successful social animals." Imitation has us learn skills; it leads to liking others and to more smooth and pleasant social interactions, and is increased when people are focused on social rather than personal cues.

Tarde's psychology of social imitation also differed from Durkheim in that rather than having ideas internalized by individuals from a vague cultural cognitive system, they were internalized by exposure to other individuals. Both Tarde and Durkheim believed that imitation was largely non-conscious (Sykes, 2010). Society and cultural change, according to Tarde (1903 [1890]), was at its core a combination of creative invention and social imitation. Invention was merely the creative fusion of older ideas, which were then absorbed by others through imitation, suggestion, and contagion. French intellectuals during Tarde's time were especially interested in extending the findings concerning hysteria, viewed as a "mimetic disease," and hypnosis to how society works more generally, including the understanding of crime (Valsiner & van der Veer, 2000, p. 43). Imitation was strongly debated as being a central force of social transmission.

Durkheim posited that social structures or facts that are exterior to the individual shape collective behavior. There was no place for psychology.

Problems in social integration and regulation thus caused suicide. Tarde, on the other hand, linked the individual with society. According to Tarde, "social relations are essentially imitative relationships," wrote Clark in an earlier revival volume on Tarde (Clark, 1969, p. 16). Society was made up of individual members, not just of social structures independent of individuals. These members made up society rather than the other way around as Durkheim saw it. Clark (1969) saw the similarity between Durkheim and Tarde in their social theory that included the actor moving toward specific goals, restricted by environmental conditions but able to use other means toward those goals, within particular institutionalized norms. Tarde attended more to individual differences and to the internalization of norms. Internalization is a psychological process. Beliefs and desires were the psychological characteristics essential for imitation and social logic (Tarde, 1903): "*Croyances par un coté, desires par l'autre*" (beliefs on one side, desires on the other) (Tarde, 1904, p. 292). Imitation took place when there was a conviction in the belief. Sentiments and desires were "almost unconscious through repetition" (Tarde, 1969, p. 187). While Tarde had a difficult time defining beliefs and desires, Graeber (2007, p. 68) reviews theories of desire and finds desire as lack, rooted in the imagination, directed toward a social relation, and seeming to "seize us from outside our conscious control."

Although Tarde did not write about suicide, suicide could be seen as imitative behavior internalized from a culture's normative attitudes toward suicide. He wrote about imitation being influenced by prestige, such as celebrity suicide being imitated in media contagion (Tarde, 1903). Tarde did not address culture directly, although his writing is certainly about culture, and the internalization of normative attitudes is only implied by Durkheim. Tarde would have agreed with the research on suicide media contagion. He saw newspapers as a powerful medium of social and personal influence (Clark, 1969). Tarde's contribution to the study of social deviance was criminology, believing that criminal acts were contagious (Barry, 2010). Tarde was popular in the early twentieth century, especially with American social scientists. Interest declined when he was perceived to have lost the debate with Durkheim and as being unscientific. Durkheim represented the popular Cartesianism, reason and order, while Tarde was with the opposing Spontaneity, which included artistic creation, personal invention and agency, and romantic subjectivism (Clark, 1969). For Tarde invention or agency is the "very texture" of the process of imitation, working not from the outside in, which Durkheim argued, but from the inside out (Karsenti, 2010, p. 59). There is currently a revival of Tarde's theory (Alliez, 2004; Katz, 2006; Niezen, 2014, in press). Yet again the inside and outside, mind and culture, are mutually constituted. Latour (2010, p. 158) argues that Tarde was indeed more scientific than Durkheim and that he was "one century ahead of his time." In a recent volume on Tarde, Candea (2010, p. 14) finds that contemporary thinkers find Tarde "sharply evocative, even mesmerizing," useful for contemporary social theory.

Diffusion

The diffusionist school in anthropology in the early twentieth century is the discipline's closest theory to that of Tarde's. It was primarily a specialization in Germany, Eastern Europe, and Russia, less so in British and French anthropology (Eriksen & Nielsen, 2001). Contrasting with evolutionism and the idea of the independent invention of culture, where different populations would have a propensity to develop similar ideas and artifacts at different rates, diffusionism held that ideas and artifacts were transmitted across populations. Originating in the philological tradition of the eighteenth century that tried to understand the spread of Indo-European languages, diffusionism became popular among German and Austrian geographers/anthropologists of the late nineteenth century and then in Britain until about 1930 (Barnard, 2000). It was a way of explaining similarities across disparate cultures. Some anthropologists, e.g., Morgan and Tylor, tried to integrate diffusionism and independent invention as interest moved from how ideas spread to where they originated. Diffusionists were losing credibility to the new functionalism in Britain by about 1920, however, primarily because they were looking at culture's origins. Anthropologists were also swayed by Durkheim. Some extremists in England tried to locate the origin of culture in Egypt, leading to accusations of "culture-theft" and contributing to the rejection and some ridicule of diffusionism (Harris, 1999; see Elliot Smith, 1927). Spinden (1927, p. 54) was not alone when he referred to diffusionist ideas as "flights of childish adventure."

The diffusion-independent invention controversy was thus doomed to failure because of its focus on the *origin* of culture, coming at a time when there was still considerable intellectual interest in the beginnings of cultural institutions. Yet by the time it was already buried in the mid-twentieth century, Evans-Pritchard had argued that diffusionism was underappreciated in British anthropology (Layton, 1997). Even Kroeber (1940) identified a need to understand the process of diffusion better, studying fashion to describe cultural patterns, and Boas encouraged anthropologists to think about diffusion as a reason for culture change (Erickson & Murphy, 2013). Boas saw culture as a mental phenomenon. In North America, diffusionism influenced the development of culture-area studies and regional comparisons, yet it was downplayed except for some quarters of archeology trying to account for cultural origin and change (Kuklick, 1996; Trigger, 1994; Renfrew, 1987). It was an important theory in Eastern European and Russian anthropology, and still maintains influence in the latter (Eriksen & Nielsen, 2001). Barnard

(2000, p. 59) writes that diffusionism is currently the least popular theory in social-cultural anthropology, yet "one of the most interesting sets of ideas anthropology has produced." Globalization studies today bears the most similarity to diffusionism, with little if any acknowledgment of this in the literature (Barnard, 2000; Eriksen & Nielsen, 2001).

The fading of diffusionism in anthropology may have been an example of the proverbial baby thrown out with the bathwater. Understanding the *process* of cultural influence and determination is an important area of research in anthropology. Michael Herzfeld (2001, p. 141) argues that cultures are mixed within all of us at many levels. He suggests that the old diffusionism might have shed light on our current understanding of culture had there been a look at how "ideas, practices and artifacts may spread through social contacts across the surface of the earth according to quite diverse logics, accumulating very different histories."

Mimesis as a central mechanism to how culture works has received some attention in recent years. Cantwell (1993, p. 6) wrote that mimesis is "the figuring-forth or summoning up that produces our elite and popular culture of literature, fine art, film, music, and so on, the area of artistic illusion . . . *ethnomimesis* is, in effect, my word for culture . . . culture is essentially imaginative." Gebauer and Wulf (1995, p. 76) argue that "all individuals . . . are shaped by mimetic processes." Donald (2005) has different definitions of mimicry, imitation, and mimesis, but here I am using them synonymously because they are so similar. Taussig (1993, p. xiii) wrote of "the nature that culture uses to create second nature, the faculty to copy, imitate, make models, explore difference, yield into and become Other." Willerslev (2007, p. 106) calls this mimetic empathy, "to put oneself imaginatively in the place of another, reproducing in one's own imagination the other's perspective." While some psychologists in the early years of the discipline were writing about the mental life of crowds, following Tarde, other writers have begun to develop notions of how ideas spread and make up who we are collectively (e.g., Colligan, Pennebaker, & Murphy, 1982; Rudé, 1995 [1981]; Schank & Abelson, 1977; Thomson, 1999). Balkin (1998) has used the idea of software to describe the transmission of ideas as cultural evolution, and there has even been some popular writing about culture change as a series of social epidemics whereby people become infected with ideas that take hold of a population after being set off rather suddenly, often dramatically. We live in worlds of "the culture of the copy," according to Schwartz (1996), where simulation supersedes duplication yet is apparent in all human affairs.

It is no surprise that, in our culture today, mimesis has for some reason become a biological reification. The last few years have seen an increase in writing about *memes*, after Dawkins' (2016) coined the term to describe the meme as a replicator, like a gene, propagated via imitation and used as the explanation of cultural transmission of ideas. Dawkins (2016, p. 249) had a meme as "a unit of cultural transmission . . . memes propagate in the meme pool by leaping from brain to brain via a process which, in the broad sense, can be called imitation." Memes are literal units of culture that, like genes, are invisible, yet become physically embodied in the human brain. Philosopher Daniel Dennett (1993)believes that mimetic evolution contributes, along with genetic evolution and phenotypic plasticity, to the structure of human conscious-ness. According to Dennet's "meme's-eye view," the "human mind is itself an artifact created when memes restructure a human brain in order to make it a better habitat for memes" (p. 207). Susan Blackmore (1999) further presents memes in the context of evolution, and discusses reli-gion and even the self as "memeplexes." Recent critics of what I would call this "biomimetic" mimetics provide more coherent argumentation than do these meme theorists. In keeping with the older definition of mimetics, commonly identified problems are that (a) memes as ideas are never literally copied as per a fax machine; (b) memes as ideas cannot be contained in discrete units, as ideas are never isolated from other ideas; (c) if memes and non-biological elements of culture like ideas, idioms, rituals, and recipes are passed on across people to shape and re-shape culture, then this is old news for anthropology; and (d) as has also been long known in anthropology, particular settings and people will play a major part in how much an idea will take hold (Bloch, 2000; Kuper, 2000; Sperber, 2000). Bloch (2000) accuses these mimeticists of ignorance of anthropology, noting that had they become familiar with the seminal writings in the history of the discipline, especially concern-ing diffusionism, they would have little if anything to say. I would second this.

Mechanisms of emotional contagion and synchrony across people have been identified (Hatfield, Cacioppo, & Rapson, 1994; Parkinson, 2011). Research supports that imitation is thus central to human development, the ability to understand other minds, language, relationships, and social life in general (Berger, 2013; Hurley & Chater, 2005b; Nehaniv & Dauten-hahn, 2007). Even William James (1904, p. 408) found imitation to be a very human thing, writing,

> And there is the imitative tendency which shows itself in large masses of men, and produces panics, and orgies, and frenzies of violence, and which only the rarest individuals can actively withstand. . . . It is particularly hard not to imitate gaping, laughing, or looking and running in a certain direction, if we see others doing so.

Ideas, according to Hacking (1999, p. 127), are "made and molded," are out there in public in social settings. Ideas can become normative. Norms are both ideational and behavioral, as in behavioral regularities seen collectively as appropriate. Norms can be internalized and become an "oughtness," something that should be done. Some norms are more accepted than others. Norms are more likely to be internalized if they are ambiguous or vague, allowing for flexibility in choice (Hechter & Opp, 2001).

Acceptability of Suicide

Can the idea of suicide be accepted as something one could do? Is acceptability of suicide a component of suicide? Attitudes toward suicide have been studied. Renberg and Jacobsson (2003) found that permissive attitudes toward suicide were associated with suicidal behavior, especially in young women. Adolescents exposed to suicidal behavior of others have more accepting attitudes toward suicide (Stein, Witztum, Brom, DeNour, & Elizur, 1992), and this exposure is associated with being more suicidal (Burke et al., 2010; Hawton, Rodham, Evans, & Weatherall, 2002; Swanson & Coleman, 2013; Wong, Stewart, Ho, & Lam, 2005). One study found that among male college students, having positive attitudes toward suicide created a link between their hopelessness and depressive symptoms and suicidal ideation (Gibb, Andover, & Beach, 2006). Another study of a very large sample found that adolescents and young adults who believe it is acceptable to end one's life were 14 times more likely to make a plan to kill themselves than those who do not have such beliefs (Joe, Romer, & Jamieson, 2007). However, the more accepting people are, the more likely they are to report, and under-reporting may take place in countries where suicide is taboo (Staples, 2012). This will be part of the internalization of the idea of suicide, accepting it as something that is possible, even desirable under some circumstances. We in the West are increasingly seeing the acceptability of physician-assisted suicide, for example. There is an ambiguity or vagueness about suicide that may make it more acceptable. Under what conditions is it acceptable? Is it sometimes bad, sometimes good? This may be part of the ambivalence and ambiguity of suicide (Shneidman, 1985).

In my research on Inuit suicide in Arctic Canada, both youth and elders say that suicidal youth are copying each other. Arctic Inuit youth have one of the highest suicide rates globally. Inuit youth have said that they want to be with their friend or relative who died by suicide. The primary trigger for suicide is breaking up with a girlfriend or boyfriend. When asked what they would do if they had such a breakup, many youth indicated they would think of suicide. It is what comes to their minds because it is so common (Kral, 2012, 2013). Widger (2012) also found unrequited or lost love to be behind suicidal youth in Sri Lanka. He writes that for some people, "suicide becomes a legitimate option" (Widger, 2012, p. 114), and believes that knowledge about suicide is transmitted as cultural knowledge (Widger, 2015).

In anthropology it is believed that most systems of meaning are culturally acquired (D'Andrade, 1984). Cultural acquisition begins in childhood, and as Rosaldo (1984, p. 140) has noted, "cultural patterns . . . provide a template for all human action, growth, and understanding." Cultural models or schemas provide motivational directions (D'Andrade & Strauss, 1992; Munro et al., 1997), have "directive force," and "set the directions of our thoughts and expectations" (Rorty, 1995, p. 216). D'Andrade (1992a) indicated that cultural models are internalized and become highly salient to the individual, held with conviction both cognitively and emotionally. People "internalize different parts of the same culture in different ways" (D'Andrade, 1992, p. 41). There are cultural models of suicide: what it is, how it is done, and why people do it. These models can be internalized by some people. They can be copied. Cultural models are cognitive schemas that "can have motivational force because these models not only label and describe the world but also set forth goals (both conscious and unconscious) and elicit or include desires" (Strauss, 1992, p. 3). D'Andrade (1992) indicated that if the construct in the schema is believed to be natural and right, the motivational force behind it is enhanced. He argued that cultural models also have affective force. Schemas are organized knowledge, and in cultural models this knowledge is shared (D'Andrade, 1995; Strauss & Quinn, 1997). Tarde believed that people imitate close models, so people would select models of suicide from their culture.

Henrich (2001) proposes three types of bias in cultural transmission that dominate the process of diffusion: direct, from specific qualities of the idea or practice (for example the method of suicide); prestige, or copying people with particular attributes who are valued (such as celebrity media contagion); and conformist or copying a norm (as Inuit youth are doing in the Arctic). Suicide can fit into this in ways that have been discussed in this paper.

McCauley (1989) identified what is called groupthink (Janis, 1972), a collective internalization where unanimity is sought. Groupthink can be pathological if the need for unanimity overrides consideration of alternative courses of action, leading to poor decisions. Is groupthink behind the extremely high suicide rate of Indigenous Arctic youth? Can negative emotions influence groupthink? A similar question is whether a vulnerable person, perturbed and preoccupied with negative emotions and hopelessness, can internalize the idea of suicide. Suicide would fit thematically with negative emotions and hopelessness. Suicidal people also fit with each other. Niezen (2009, in press) has suggested that Indigenous suicidal youth feel a sense of belonging with each other, where self-destruction can be a criterion for social inclusion among some youth. Suicidal youth are drawn to each other. Niezen (in press, p. 26) calls this a "perverse sociability." This may be what Strathern (2016) refers to as relationality to an extreme. The feeling of not belonging is a suicide risk factor, and it may be that the only group the severely suicidal person feels a belonging to is other suicidal people. One of the factors contributing to media suicide contagion is identification with the suicide victim, such as demographic similarities including age, gender, marital strain, ethnicity, and citizenship (Gould, 2001; Niederkrotenthaler et al., 2009). This ties back to Tarde's law of propinquity in imitation, where people identify with similar others.

Who then is vulnerable to the idea of suicide? Suicide risk factors have been studied for many years, and much is known. Depression, substance abuse, hopelessness, agitation, being male, being non-heterosexual, being a younger Indigenous or older White male, having attempted suicide, having other mental disorders like bipolar disorder or schizophrenia, having been hospitalized for a mental disorder, unemployment, disability, having a family history of suicide, having a history of sexual abuse, and being bullied have all been identified as risk factors (Brown, Beck, Steer, & Grisham, 2000; Conwell, Duberstein, & Caine, 2002; Mościcki, 1997; Qin et al., 2003; Russell & Joyner, 2001). Yet most people with these risk factors do not kill themselves or even attempt suicide. These risk factors are forms of potential perturbation, and they do not by themselves lead to suicide. It is the perturbed person who is merely at risk. We do not know why some people who are perturbed internalize the idea of suicide. This is an area worthy of research, including the process of such internalization.

We need to see a return to diffusion theory examining not the origin but the *process* of how culture works, as argued by Sperber (1996a) and others. Suicide operates like other ideas, and this idea is transmitted culturally. Suicide thus has a commonality with fashion, perhaps more than with psychiatry (Raustiala & Sprigman, 2010). There is a vulnerable, perturbed person who has actively internalized the idea of suicide. Suicide has become salient. The cultural model will include why one would kill oneself and how one would kill oneself. In cultural transmission "an individual does not learn from another but through another" (Schönpflug, 2009b, p. 466), by taking on the model's perspective. The perturbed person for whom suicide is now salient will identify with this, with other people who have killed themselves, and will imitate how and why people in his or her culture kill themselves. Suicide methods vary culturally; people copy each other in how they kill themselves (Ajdacic-Gross et al., 2008; Lester, 2013; Liu et al., 2007; McIntosh & Santos, 1982). Suicide is thus like so many other human behaviors, imitated. And the idea of suicide is like so many other ideas, ones that spread within a cultural group. Such a perspective fits with the revival of Tarde, with his emphasis on volition, and imitation in the culture. Tarde emphasized agency with his focus on invention, conscious volition, the source of human innovation, and progress. Again, it is the process of acting and being acted upon.

6   Afterword

This book presents a new cultural theory of suicide based on imitation, contagion, diffusion, and internalization. It is a theory of cultural mimesis and transmission. Suicide is viewed as a function of perturbation and lethality or the idea of suicide. It is the decision to complete suicide that is lethal. The idea of suicide comes from our culture, and humans copy this idea into their minds. We have seen how imitative humans are in just about everything that is human, and this starts from when we are first born and continues through life. It has been found that there is media contagion in suicide, however here we look at suicide being contagious in general. It has appeared in clusters and pacts, and there have been mass suicides. Chapter 3 looks at social epidemics that have been called mass hysteria. This is one way of seeing how ideas are spread in society. There have been a great many social epidemics, in schools, workplaces, and communities. A number of cases were described, and symptoms typically include nausea, vomiting, headaches, and dizziness. Hysteria was discussed as a contagious mental disorder, a transient mental illness that has disappeared like the fugue in France or multiple personality disorder in North America. Contagion takes on many forms and affects a very large number of human behaviors, from what shoes we wear to binge eating to doctors prescribing medications. Ideas about suicide have changed quite dramatically over time, and have moved from seeing it as free will to being determined by such things as mental illness. Various theories of suicide were reviewed, and Durkheim's sociological theory of suicide was looked at in some detail, particularly his notion of collective representations and anomic and egoistic suicide. I propose that his theory of suicide is a theory of perturbation. It appears that most theories of suicide are theories of perturbation. The only theory that is a theory of lethality of suicide, besides the one in this book, is by Thomas Joiner (2005). He believes that suicidal people have what he calls accrued lethality, the learning of not to be afraid of death or pain. And this is learned, from the outside in. Culture and suicide was reviewed, looking at how suicide differs across cultures, how attitudes toward suicide are related to suicide rates, and the need for an anthropological imagination in thinking about suicide. Gabriel Tarde's theory of cultural imitation was applied to suicide, and the concept of psychological internalization was added to understand how this process operates. The mind is seen as social, as cultural. Suicide is imitated, and suicide becomes an acceptable option. My theory of suicide is presented as a new approach to suicide, as a cultural theory, a lethality theory.

That suicide is copied is known. In the news on May 18, 2017, was the story of the lead singer of the band Soundgarden Chris Cornell's suicide in Detroit after they played a concert. Cornell was found with blood running from his mouth and a red exercise band around his neck. He had struggled with substance abuse for most of his life. His family claimed that it was not suicide, that he did not know what he was doing, and that his death was caused by the drug Ativan which the singer had been taking for anxiety. Again, taking agency away from a suicide. In an article about Cornell's suicide, Fast (2017) calls it a "brain chemical suicide." She wrote that suicide is not a conscious choice but is a result of mental illness. Cornell's wife said that he had told her he was "just tired" that evening, and he was slurring his words in a final phone call (Pearce, 2017). Then two months later a close friend of his, Chester Bennington, the lead singer of the band Linkin Park, was found hanging by a belt from a hotel door. He hanged himself on Cornell's birthday and had been hit very hard by Cornell's death. He sang at Cornell's funeral. Like Cornell, he had a history of substance abuse and he had been suicidal in the past (Alexander, 2017). Singer Annie Clark, also known as St. Vincent, has a song about suicide on her new album. She said, "Like any red-blooded American, I've considered suicide" (Paumgarten, 2017, p. 4). Do many people think that thinking about suicide is so common? Has it become so acceptable? The lifetime prevalence of suicidal ideation is 9.2%, making a plan for suicide is 3.1%, and suicide attempt it is 2.7% (Nock et al., 2008). The lifetime prevalence of suicidal ideation for Australians is 10.4% (De Leo, Cerin, Spathonis, & Burgis, 2005). The lifetime prevalence of suicidal ideation for older adolescents is higher at 21.1% (Andrews & Lewinsohn, 1992). Another study found the prevalence of suicidal ideation among adolescents to be 29.9% (Evans, Hawton, Rodham, & Deeks, 2005). So suicide is not considered by every red-blooded American, but it is prevalent enough. The copying of suicide by hanging by singer Chester Bennington shows how suicide can be imitated. And St. Vincent thinks that suicidal ideation is extremely common.

The issue of free will versus determinism in suicide has been discussed. In looking at the study of crime, Burkhead (2006) outlines a continuum of choice with free will on one side and determinism on the other, and where both are active. He writes that "a person's behavior may be seen as having some element of choice and some element that is not entirely under the person's control" (p. 21). He asks where on this continuum must a behavior fall in order for the person to be held responsible? We have seen that both free will and determinism are true for suicide. This book shows a side of cultural determinism, but it is not without free will. The suicidal person makes a choice. This is the cognitive lethality of the idea of suicide as a response to perturbation.

I agree with Shneidman (1993) that suicide is multidimensional and should be studied by multiple disciplines. While this book is a needed look at culture and suicide, all perspectives need to be put forward to understand suicide. We are neurobiological beings, so there must be some neurobiology associated with being suicidal. It may be the same as that associated with being very upset. The psychology of suicide is very important and was discussed in Chapter 2. This includes the feeling of not belonging and being a burden on others, hopelessness, and deep psychological pain. The theory in this book is not only anthropological but also psychological, as the idea of suicide is cognitive. Charles Neuringer, a major researcher on cognition and suicide, indicated that cognition is "the key to dealing with suicide" (Ellis, 2006b, p. 19). Might the cognitive characteristics of being suicidal be associated with being vulnerable to internalizing the idea of suicide? Characteristics such as perceptual constriction, cognitive rigidity, or dichotomous thinking? It is possible, and research needs to look at this question and into the vulnerability to internalizing the idea of suicide in general.

Critical suicide studies is moving forward. Jaworski (2014) has a book on gender and suicide that shows how suicide must be understood through a gendered lens and that current knowledge about suicide is masculinist. She argues, "What is male in suicide is never about gender and what is female is always about gender" (p. 16). Male deaths are associated with heroism, bravery, and courage, while women's femininities do not allow them to kill themselves. Men are completers while women are attempters. Ian Marsh's (2010) book on suicide poses a significant critique of suicidology, showing how it is individualist, pathologizing, and sees itself as a science. The anthropological and cultural books on suicide have been described, and they shed very important light on suicide. The critical suicide studies group is planning a book series and more international conferences. The American Association of Suicidology now has a book award for lived experience, for people writing about their suicide attempts and ideation. Suicidology is thus changing and moving into new fields of endeavor.

This book's cultural approach to suicide fits with the new field of critical suicidology. Critical suicidology does not reject traditional suicidology, but rather expands the focus to such things as context. If suicide is a collective phenomenon, then suicide prevention can also be collective. This has been seen in a few Inuit communities in the Canadian Arctic. Kuhn (1977) wrote about the "essential tension" needed as sciences move forward. This is the case as suicidology moves forward with new theories and methodologies. Context is an important factor in suicide, one that is often overlooked other than looking at risk factors. I suggested that risk factors are merely perturbation and have nothing to do with suicide, as most people with all the risk factors will never become suicidal. It is the perturbed, upset person who is vulnerable to internalizing the idea of suicide and possibly acting on it. Seeing suicide as cultural can lead to new research, especially ethnographic research, looking closely at personal and collective meanings regarding self-destruction. Suicide does manifest itself differently in different cultures, and more comparative studies are called for. It will be important to understand the meanings of suicide in different cultures. A cultural approach will thus add significantly to critical suicidology. It is time for suicidology to widen its lens.

References

Aarts, H., Dijksterhuis, A., & Dik, G. (2008). Goal contagion: Inferring goals from others' actions—and what it leads to. In J. Y. Shah & W. L. Gardner (Eds.), *Handbook of motivation science* (pp. 265–280). New York, NY: Guilford.

Abramson, L. Y., Metalsky, G. I., & Alloy, L. B. (1989). Hopelessness depression: A theory-based subtype of depression. *Psychological Review*, *96*, 358–372.

Abrutyn, S. (2017). What Hindi Sati can teach us about the sociocultural an social psychological dynamics of suicide. *Journal of the Theory of Social Behavior*, *47*, 1–18.

Abrutyn, S., & Mueller, A. S. (2014a). The socioemotional foundations of suicide: A microsociological view of Durkheim's suicide. *Sociological Theory*, *32*, 327–351.

Abrutyn, S., & Mueller, A. S. (2014b). Are suicidal behaviors contagious in adolescence? Using longitudinal data to examine suicide suggestion. *American Sociological Review*, *79*, 211–227.

Abrutyn, S., & Mueller, A. S. (2014c). Reconsidering Durkheim's assessment of Tarde: Formalizing a Tardian theory of imitation, contagion, and suicide suggestion. *Sociological Forum*, *29*, 698–719.

Abrutyn, S., & Mueller, A. S. (2015). When too much integration and regulation hurts: Reenvisioning Durkheim's altruistic suicide. *Society and Mental Health*, *6*(1), 56–71. doi:10.1177/2156869315604346.

Abrutyn, S., & Mueller, A. S. (2018). Toward a cultural-structural theory of suicide: Examining excessive regulation and its discontents. *Sociological Theory*, *36*, 48–66.

Adams, J., & Adams, M. (1996). The association among negative life events, perceived problem-solving alternatives, depression, and suicidal ideation in adolescent psychiatric patients. *Journal of Child Psychology and Psychiatry*, *37*, 715–720.

Adams, W. Y. (1998). *The philosophical roots of anthropology*. Stanford, CA: CSLI Publications.

Ajdacic-Gross, V., Weiss, M. G., Ring, M., Hepp, U., Bopp, M., Gutzwiller, F., & Rossler, W. (2008). Methods of suicide: International suicide patterns derived from the WHO mortality database. *Bulletin of the World Health Organization*, *86*, 726–732.

Alexander, H. (2017, July 21). Chester Bennington, Linkin Park frontman, wrote open letter to dead Chris Cornell months before suicide. *The Telegraph*.

Ali-Gombe, A., Guthrie, E., & McDermott, N. (1996). Mass hysteria: One syndrome or two? *British Journal of Psychiatry, 168,* 633–635.

Allen, D. (1997). *Culture and the self: Philosophical and religious perspectives, east and west.* Boulder, CO: Westview.

Allen, F., & Gale, D. (2000). Financial contagion. *Journal of Political Economy, 108,* 1–33.

Alliez, E. (2004). The difference and repetition of Gabriel Tarde. *Scandinavian Journal of Social Theory, 5,* 49–54.

Allport, F. H. (1924). *Social psychology.* Boston, MA: Houghton Mifflin Company.

Alvarez, A. (1971). *The savage god: A study of suicide.* New York, NY: Norton.

American Psychiatric Association. (2013). *DSM-5: Diagnostic and statistical manual of mental disorders* (5th ed.). Washington, DC: American Psychiatric Publishing.

Anderson, E. N. (2011). Emotions, motivation, and behavior in cognitive anthropology. In D. B. Kronenfeld, G. Bennardo, V. C. de Munch, & M. D. Fischer (Eds.), *A companion to cognitive anthropology* (pp. 314–330). West Sussex, UK: Wiley-Blackwell.

Andrews, J. A., & Lewinsohn, P. M. (1992). Suicidal attempts among older adolescents: Prevalence and co-occurrence with psychiatric disorders. *Journal of the American Academy of Child and Adolescent Psychiatry, 31,* 655–662.

Anestis, M. D., & Houtsma, C. (2018). The association between gun ownership and statewide overall suicide rates. *Suicide and Life-Threatening Behavior, 48,* 204–217.

Anestis, M. D., Khazem, L. R., Law, K. C., Houtsma, C., LeTard, R., Moberg, F., & Martin, R. (2015). The association between state laws regulating handgun ownership and statewide suicide rates. *American Journal of Public Health, 105,* 2059–2067.

Angell, M. (2011a, June 23). The epidemic of mental illness: Why? *New York Review of Books.*

Angell, M. (2011b, July 14). The illusions of psychiatry. *The New York Review of Books.*

Anisfeld, B. E. (2005). What does infant imitation tell us about the underlying representations? In S. Hurley & N. Chater (Eds.), *Perspectives on imitation: From neuroscience to social science. Volume 2: Imitation, human development, and culture* (pp. 191–194). Cambridge, MA: MIT Press.

Article I (no author). (1844). Definition of insanity—Nature of the disease. *The American Journal of Insanity, 1,* 97–116.

Article IV (no author). (1845). Cases of insanity—Illustrating the importance of early treatment in preventing suicide. *The American Journal of Insanity, 1,* 243–249.

Åsberg, M., Träskman, L., & Thorén, P. (1976). 5-HIAA in the cerebrospinal fluid: A biochemical suicide predictor? *Archives of General Psychiatry, 33,* 1193–1197.

Bachman, R., & Strauss, M. A. (1992). *Death and violence on the reservation: Homicide, family violence, and suicide in American Indian populations.* New York, NY: Praeger.

Baechler, J. (1985). *Suicides* (B. Cooper, Trans.). New York, NY: Basic.

Baker, E. W. (2015). *A storm of witchcraft: The Salem trials and the American experience.* New York, NY: Oxford University Press.

Balaratnasinggam, S., & Janca, A. (2006). Mass hysteria revisited. *Current Opinion in Psychiatry, 19,* 171–174.

Baldessarini, R. J., & Hennen, J. (2004). Genetics of suicide: An overview. *Harvard Review of Psychiatry, 12,* 1–13.

Balikci, A. (1970). *The Netsilik Eskimo.* New York, NY: Doubleday.

Balkin, J. M. (1998). *Cultural software: A theory of ideology.* New Haven, CT: Yale University Press.

Baller, R. D., & Richardson, K. K. (2009). The "dark side" of the strength of weak ties: The diffusion of suicidal thoughts. *Journal of Health and Social Behavior, 50,* 261–276.

Bandura, A. (2001). Social learning theory of mass communication. *Mediapsychology, 3,* 265–299.

Bangalore, S., & Messerli, F. H. (2013). Gun ownership and firearm-related deaths. *The American Journal of Medicine, 126,* 873–876.

Bantes, J., & Swartz, L. (2017). The cultural turn in suicidology: What can we claim and what do we know? *Death Studies, 8,* 512–520.

Barbagli, M. (2015). *Farewell to the world: A history of suicide.* Malden, MA: Polity.

Barnard, A. (2000). *History and theory in anthropology.* Cambridge, UK: Cambridge University Press.

Barry, A. (2010). Tarde's method: Between statistics and experimentation. In M. Candea (Ed.), *The social after Gabriel Tarde: Debates and assessments* (pp. 177–190). London, UK: Routledge.

Bar-Tal, D. (2000). *Shared beliefs in a society: Social psychological analysis.* Thousand Oaks, CA: Sage.

Bartholomew, R. E., & Rickard, B. (2014). *Mass hysteria in schools: A worldwide history since 1566.* Jefferson, NC: McFrarland & Company.

Bateson, J. (2012). *The final leap: Suicide on the Golden Gate Bridge.* Berkeley, CA: University of California Press.

Baumeister, R. F. (1990). Suicide as escape from self. *Psychological Review, 97,* 90–113.

Baumeister, R. F., & Landau, M. J. (2018). Finding the meaning of meaning: Emerging insights on four grand questions. *Review of General Psychology, 22,* 1–10.

Baumeister, R. F., & Leary, M. R. (1995). The need to belong: Desire for interpersonal attachments as a fundamental human motivation. *Psychological Bulletin, 117,* 497–529.

Bearman, P., & Moody, J. (2004). Suicide and friendships among American adolescents. *American Journal of Public Health, 94,* 89–95.

Beautrais, A. (2007). Suicide by jumping. *Crisis, 28,* 58–63.

Bechtel, W. (2009). Explanation: Mechanism, modularity, and situated cognition. In P. Robbins & M. Aydede (Eds.), *The Cambridge handbook of situated cognition* (pp. 155–170). New York, NY: Cambridge University Press.

Bechtold, D. (1988). Cluster suicide in American Indian adolescents. *American Indian and Alaska Native Mental Health Research, 1,* 26–35.

Beck, A. T. (1967). *Depression: Causes and treatment.* Philadelphia, PA: University of Pennsylvania Press.

Beck, A. T. (1987). Cognitive models of depression. *Journal of Cognitive Psychotherapy, 1*, 2–27.

Beck, A. T., Brown, G., & Steer, R. A. (1989). Prediction of eventual suicide in psychiatric inpatients by clinical ratings of hopelessness. *Journal of Consulting and Clinical Psychology, 57*, 309–310.

Beck, A. T., Steer, R. A., Kovacs, M., & Garrison, B. (1985). Hopelessness and eventual suicide: A 10-year prospective study of patients hospitalized with suicidal ideation. *American Journal of Psychiatry, 142*, 559–563.

Beck, A. T., Weissman, A., Lester, D., & Trexler, L. (1974). The measurement of pessimism: The hopelessness scale. *Journal of Consulting and Clinical Psychology, 42*, 861–865.

Behere, P. B., & Bhise, M. C. (2009). Farmers' suicide: Across culture. *Indian Journal of Psychiatry, 51*, 242–243.

Bell, R. (2012). *We shall be no more: Suicide and self-government in the newly United States.* Cambridge, MA: Harvard University Press.

Bellisari, A. (2013). *The obesity epidemic in America: Connecting biology and culture.* Long Grove, IL: Waveland Press.

Benedict, R. (1953). Continuities and discontinuities in cultural conditioning. In C. Kluckhohn & H. A. Murray (Eds.), *Personality in nature, society, and culture* (pp. 522–531). New York, NY: Alfred A. Knopf.

Bentley, A., Earls, M., & O'Brien, M. J. (2011). *I'll have what she's having: Mapping social behavior.* Cambridge, MA: MIT Press.

Berger, J. (2013). *Contagious: Why things catch on.* New York, NY: Simon & Schuster.

Bergmans, Y., Rowe, A., Dineen, M., & Johnson, D. (2016). When despair and hope meet the stigma of "manipulation" and "ambivalence." In J. White, I. Marsh, M. J. Kral, & J. Morris (Eds.), *Critical suicidology: Transforming suicide research and prevention for the 21st century* (pp. 133–153). Vancouver, BC: University of British Columbia Press.

Berlin, I. N. (1987). Suicide among American Indian adolescents: An overview. *Suicide and Life-Threatening Behavior, 17*, 218–232.

Berry, J. W., & Georgas, J. (2009). An ecocultural perspective on cultural transmission: The family across cultures. In U. Schönpflug (Ed.), *Cultural transmission: Psychological, developmental, social, and methodological aspects* (pp. 95–125). New York, NY: Cambridge University Press.

Berry, J. W., Poortinga, Y. H., Segall, M. H., & Dasen, P. R. (1992). *Cross-cultural psychology: Research and applications.* New York, NY: Cambridge University Press.

Bertolote, J. M., & Fleischmann, A. (2002). Correspondence: Suicide rates in China. *The Lancet, 359*, 2274.

Besnard, P. (2002). Suicide and anomie. In. W. S. F. Pickering (Ed.), *Durkheim today* (pp. 81–85). New York, NY: Berghahn.

Best, J. (2006). *Flavor of the month: Why smart people fall for fads.* Berkeley, CA: University of California Press.

Bikhchandani, S., Hirshleifer, D., & Welch, I. (1992). A theory of fads, fashion, custom, and cultural change as informational cascades. *Journal of Political Economy, 100*, 992–1025.

Bjerregaard, P., & Curtis, T. (2002). Culture change and mental health in Greenland: The association of childhood conditions, language, and urbanization with mental health and suicidal thoughts among the Inuit of Greenland. *Social Science and Medicine, 54,* 33–48.

Blackman, L., & Walkerdine, V. (2001). *Mass hysteria: Critical psychology and media studies.* New York, NY: Palgrave.

Blackmore, S. (1999). *The meme machine.* Oxford, UK: Oxford University Press.

Blair-West, G. W., Cantor, C. H., Mellsop, G. W., & Eyeson-Annan, M. L. (1999). Lifetime suicide risk in major depression: Sex and age determinants. *Journal of Affective Disorders, 55,* 171–178.

Blasco-Fontecilla, H. (2012). On suicide clusters: More than contagion. *Australian and New Zealand Journal of Psychiatry, 46,* 1–2.

Bloch, M. (2000). A well-disposed social anthropologist's problems with memes. In R. Aunger (Ed.), *Darwinizing culture: The status of memetics as a science* (pp. 189–203). Oxford, UK: Oxford University Press.

Bloch, M. (2005). *Essays on cultural transmission.* Oxford, UK: Berg.

Bloch, M. (2012). *Anthropology and the cognitive challenge.* New York, NY: Cambridge University Press.

Bloor, D. (2001 [2000]). Collective representations as social institutions. In W. S. F. Pickering (Ed.), *Emile Durkheim: Critical assessments of leading sociologists* (Vol. 2, pp. 385–395). London, UK: Routledge.

Blumen, L. (2010). *Bullying epidemic: Not just child's play.* Toronto, ON: Camberley Press.

Boas, F. (2013). *Psychological problems in anthropology.* London, UK: Read Books. Originally published in 1910.

Boergers, J., Spirito, A., & Donaldson, D. (1998). Reasons for adolescent suicide attempts: Associations with psychological functioning. *Journal of the American Academy of Child and Adolescent Psychiatry, 37,* 1287–1293.

Bollas, C. (2000). *Hysteria.* New York, NY: Routledge.

Bondy, B., Buettner, A., & Zill, P. (2006). Genetics of suicide. *Molecular Psychiatry, 11,* 336–351.

Booth, H. (2010). The evolution of epidemic suicide on Guam: Context and contagion. *Suicide and Life-Threatening Behavior, 40,* 1–13.

Boss, L. P. (1997). Epidemic hysteria: A review of the published literature. *Epidemiologic Reviews, 19,* 233–243.

Boyce, N. (2011). Suicide clusters: The undiscovered country. *The Lancet, 378,* 1452.

Boyer, P., & Nissenbaum, S. (1974). *Salem possessed: The social origins of witchcraft.* Cambridge, MA: Harvard University Press.

Breault, K. D. (1994). Was Durkheim right? A critical survey of the empirical literature on *Le Suicide.* In D. Lester (Ed.), *Emile Durkheim: Le suicide 100 years later* (pp. 11–29). Philadelphia, PA: The Charles Press.

Breault, K. D., & Kposowa, A. J. (2000). Social integration and marital status: A multi-variate individual-level study of 30,157 suicides. In W. S. F. Pickering & G. Walford (Eds.), *Durkheim's Suicide: A century of research and debate* (pp. 156–179). London, UK: Routledge.

Brent, D. A., & Bridge, J. (2003). Firearms availability and suicide: Evidence, interventions, and future directions. *American Behavioral Scientist, 46,* 1192–1210.

Brent, D. A., & Melhem, N. (2008). Familial transmission of suicidal behavior. *Psychiatric Clinics of North America, 31,* 157–177.

Brent, D. A., Oquendo, M., Birmaher, B., Greenhill, L., Kolko, D., Stanley, B., Zelazny, J., Brodsky, B., Firinciogullari, S., Ellis, S. P., & Mann, J. J. (2003).

Peripubertal suicide attempts in offspring of suicide attempters with siblings concordant for suicidal behavior. *American Journal of Psychiatry, 160,* 1061–1070.

Breuer, J., & Freud, S. (1957). *Studies on hysteria.* New York, NY: Basic. Originally published in 1895.

Brewer, M. B., & Yuki, M. (2007). Culture and social identity. In S. Kitayama & D. Cohen (Eds.), *Handbook of cultural psychology* (pp. 307–322). New York, NY: Guilford.

Brezo, J., Klempan, T., & Turecki, G. (2008). The genetics of suicide: A critical review of molecular studies. *Psychiatric Clinics of North America, 31,* 179–203.

Bromley, D. G., & Melton, J. G. (Eds.). (2002). *Cults, religion, and violence.* New York, NY: Cambridge University Press.

Brown, G. K., Beck, A. T., Steer, R. A., & Grisham, J. R. (2000). Risk factors for suicide in psychiatric outpatients: A 20-year prospective study. *Journal of Consulting and Clinical Psychology, 68,* 371–377.

Broz, L., & Münster, D. (Eds.). (2016). *Suicide and agency: Anthropological perspectives on self-destruction, personhood, and power.* Burlington, VT: Ashgate.

Bruner, J. (1990). *Acts of meaning.* Cambridge, MA: Harvard University Press.

Burke, A. K., Galfalvy, H., Everett, B., Currier, D., Zelazny, J., Oquendo, M. A., . . . & Brent, D. A. (2010). Effect of exposure to suicidal behavior on suicide attempt in a high-risk sample of offspring of depressed parents. *Journal of the American Academy of Child and Adolescent Psychiatry, 49,* 114–121.

Burke, P. (2005). *History and social theory.* Ithaca, NY: Cornell University Press.

Burkhead, M. D. (2006). *The search for the causes of crime.* Jefferson, NC: McFarland & Company.

Burt, R. S. (1987). Social contagion and innovation: Cohesion versus structural equivalence. *American Journal of Sociology, 92,* 1287–1335.

Burton, R. (2001 [1621]). *The anatomy of melancholy.* New York, NY: New York Review of Books.

Calvo, G. A., & Mendoza, E. G. (2000). Rational contagion and the globalization of securities markets. *Journal of International Economics, 51,* 79–113.

Campos, R. C., Gomes, M., Holden, R. R., Piteira, M., & Rainha, A. (2017). Does psychache mediate the relationship between general distress and suicidal ideation? *Death Studies, 41,* 241–245.

Camus, A. (1955). *The myth of Sisyphus and other essays.* New York, NY: Vintage.

Candea, M. (2010). Revisiting Tarde's house. In M. Candea (Ed.), *The social after Gabriel Tarde: Debates and assessments* (pp. 1–24). London, UK: Routledge.

Canetto, S. S. (2008). Women and suicidal behavior: A cultural analysis. *American Journal of Orthopsychiatry, 78,* 259–266.

Cantwell, R. (1993). *Ethnomimesis: Folklife and the representation of culture.* Chapel Hill, NC: University of North Carolina Press.

Caron, J. (2010). Gun control and suicide: Possible impact of Canadian legislation to ensure safe storage of firearms. *Archives of Suicide Research, 8,* 361–374.

Carrington, P. J., & Moyer, S. (1994). Gun availability and suicide in Canada: Testing the displacement hypothesis. *Studies on Crime and Crime Prevention, 3,* 168–178.

Carver, C. S., & Scheier, M. F. (2002). Optimism. In C. R. Snyder & S. J. Lopez (Eds.), *Handbook of positive psychology* (pp. 231–243). Oxford, UK: Oxford University Press.

Casper, S. T. (2016). The political without guarantees: Contagious police shootings, neuroscientific cultural imaginaries, and neuroscientific futures. In K. Nixon & L. Servitje (Eds.), *Endemic: Essays in contagion theory* (pp. 169–190). London, UK: Palgrave MacMillan.

Casson, R. W. (1983). Schemata in cognitive anthropology. *Annual Review of Anthropology, 12*, 429–462.

Cátedra, M. (1992). *This world, other worlds: Sickness, suicide, death, and the afterlife among the Vaqueiros de Alzada of Spain.* Chicago, IL: University of Chicago Press.

Celinska, K. (2007). Individualism and collectivism in America: The case of gun ownership and attitudes toward gun control. *Sociological Perspectives, 50*, 229–247.

Cerulo, K. A. (2002). Establishing a sociology of culture and cognition. In K. A. Cerulo (Ed.), *Culture in mind: Toward a sociology of culture and cognition* (pp. 1–19). New York, NY: Routledge.

Champion, F. P., & Taylor, R. (1963). Mass hysteria associated with insect bites. *Journal of the South Carolina Medical Association, 59*, 351–353.

Chandler, M. J., & Lalonde, C. (1998). Cultural continuity as a hedge against suicide in Canada's First Nations. *Transcultural Psychiatry, 35*, 191–219.

Chang, S.-S., Gunnell, D., Wheeler, B. W., Yip, P., & Sterne, J. A. C. (2010). The evolution of the epidemic of charcoal-burning suicide in Taiwan: A spatial and temporal analysis. *PLOS Medicine, 7*, 1–10.

Chaplin, J. P. (2015). *Rumor, fear and the madness of crowds.* Mineola, NY: Dover Publications.

Chavez-Hernandez, A.-M., Paramo, D., Leenaars, A. A., & Leenaars, L. (2006). Suicide notes in Mexico: What do they tell us? *Suicide and Life-Threatening Behavior, 36*, 709–715.

Cheng, Q., Hong, L., Silenzio, V., & Caine, E. D. (2014). Suicide contagion: A systematic review of definitions and research utility. *PLoS ONE, 9*(9), e108724.

Chirkov, V. I., Ryan, R. M., & Willness, C. (2005). Cultural context and psychological needs in Canada and Brazil: Testing a self-determination approach to the internalization of cultural practices, identity, and well-being. *Journal of Cross-Cultural Psychology, 36*, 423–443.

Chotai, J., Renberg, E. S., & Jacobson, L. (1999). Season of birth associated with age and method of suicide. *Archives of Suicide Research, 5*, 245–254.

Christakis, N. A., & Fowler, J. H. (2011). Contagion in prescribing behavior among networks of doctors. *Marketing Science, 30*, 213–216.

Chryssides, G. D. (2011). Approaching heaven's gate. In G. D. Chryssides (Ed.), *Heaven's gate: Postmodernity and popular culture in a suicide group* (pp. 1–15). Burlington, VT: Ashgate.

Chu, J. P., Goldblum, P., Floyd, R., & Bongar, B. (2010). The cultural theory and model of suicide. *Applied and Preventive Psychology, 14*, 25–40.

Clark, T. N. (Ed.). (1969). *Gabriel Tarde: On communication and social influence.* Chicago, IL: University of Chicago Press.

Clarke, R. V., & Lester, D. (1989). *Suicide: Closing the exits.* New York, NY: Springer-Verlag.

Cohen, D. A. (2014). *A big fat crisis: The hidden forces behind the obesity epidemic and how we can end it.* New York, NY: Nation Books.

Cole, D. A. (1989). Psychopathology of adolescent suicide: Hopelessness, coping beliefs, and depression. *Journal of Abnormal Psychology, 98*, 248–255.

Cole, M., & Sylvia, S. (1974). *Culture and thought: A psychological introduction.* New York, NY: Wiley.

Coleman, L. (2004). *The copycat effect: How the media and popular culture trigger the mayhem in tomorrow's headlines.* New York, NY: Paraview.

Colligan, M. J., & Murphy, L. R. (1982). A review of mass psychogenic illness in work settings. In M. J. Colligan, J. W. Pennebaker, & L. R. Murphy (Eds.), *Mass psychogenic illness: A social psychological analysis* (pp. 33–52). Hillsdale, NJ: Lawrence Erlbaum.

Colligan, M. J., Pennebaker, J. W., & Murphy, L. R. (Eds.). (1982). *Mass psychogenic illness: A social psychological analysis.* Hillsdale, NJ: Erlbaum.

Collins, W. A., Gleason, T., & Semsa Jr., A. (1997). Internalization, autonomy, and relationships: Development during adolescence. In J. E. Grusec & L. Kuczynski (Eds.), *Parenting and children's internalization of values: A handbook of contemporary theory* (pp. 78–99). New York, NY: Wiley.

Colt, G. H. (1991). *The enigma of suicide.* New York, NY: Touchstone.

Colucci, E. (2013). Cultural meaning(s) of suicide: A cross-cultural study. In E. Colucci & D. Lester (Eds.), *Suicide and culture: Understanding the context* (pp. 93–196). Boston, MA: Hogrefe.

Colucci, E., & Lester, D. (2013). *Suicide and culture: Understanding the context.* Boston, MA: Hogrefe.

Colucci, E., Too, L. S., & Minas, H. (2017). A suicide research agenda for people from immigrant and refugee backgrounds. *Death Studies, 41*(8), 502–511.

Conner, K. R., Duberstein, P. R., Conwell, Y., Seidlitz, L., & Caine, E. D. (2001). Psychological vulnerability to completed suicide: A review of empirical studies. *Suicide and Life-Threatening Behavior, 31,* 367–385.

Conwell, Y., Duberstein, P. R., & Caine, E. D. (2002). Risk factors for suicide in later life. *Biological Psychiatry, 52,* 193–204.

Counts, D. (1991). Suicide in different ages from a cross-cultural perspective. In A. A. Leenaars (Ed.), *Life-span perspectives of suicide: Time-lines in the suicide process* (pp. 215–230). New York, NY: Plenum.

Cover, R. (2016). Queer youth suicide: Discourses of difference, framing suicidality, and the regimentation of identity. In J. White, I. Marsh, M. J. Kral, & J. Morris (Eds.), *Critical suicidology: Transforming suicide research and prevention for the 21st century* (pp. 188–208). Vancouver, BC: University of British Columbia Press.

Crandall, C. S. (1988). Social contagion of binge eating. *Journal of Personality and Social Psychology, 55,* 588–598.

Crozier, I. (2018). Introduction: Pow Meng Yap and the culture-bound syndromes. *History of Psychiatry, 29,* 363–385.

Cummings, P., Koepsell, T. D., Grossman, D. C., Savarino, J., & Thompson, R. S. (2011). The association between the purchase of a handgun and homicide or suicide. *American Journal of Public Health, 87,* 974–978.

D'Andrade, R. G. (1984). Cultural meaning systems. In R. A. Shweder & R. A. Levine (Eds.), *Culture theory: Essays on mind, self, and emotion* (pp. 88–119). Cambridge, UK: Cambridge University Press.

D'Andrade, R. G. (1995). *The development of cognitive anthropology.* New York, NY: Cambridge University Press.

D'Andrade, R. G. (1992a). Schemas and motivation. In R. D'Andrade & C. Strauss (Eds.), *Human motives and cultural models* (pp. 23–44). New York, NY: Cambridge University Press.

D'Andrade, R. G. (1992b). Afterword. In R. D'Andrade & C. Strauss (Eds.), *Human motives and cultural models* (pp. 225–232). New York, NY: Cambridge University Press.

D'Andrade, R. G., & Strauss, C. (1992). *Human motives and cultural models.* Cambridge, UK: Cambridge University Press.

Dawes, G. (2014). Forward. In R. E. Bartholomew & B. Rickard (Eds.), *Mass hysteria in schools: A worldwide history since 1566* (p. 1). Jefferson, NC: McFarland & Company.

Dawkins, R. (2016). *The selfish gene* (4th ed.). Oxford, UK: Oxford University Press.

Dean, P. J., & Range, L. M. (1999). Testing the escape theory of suicide in an outpatient clinical population. *Cognitive Therapy and Research, 23,* 561–572.

Dean, P. J., Range, L. M., & Goggin, W. C. (1996). The escape theory of suicide in college students: Testing a model that includes perfectionism. *Suicide and Life-Threatening Behavior, 26,* 181–186.

Deci, E. L., Eghrari, H., Patrick, B. C., & Leone, D. R. (1994). Facilitating internalization: The self-determination theory perspective. *Journal of Personality, 62,* 119–142.

De Leo, D., Cerin, E., Spathonis, K., & Burgis, S. (2005). Life time risk of suicidal ideation and attempts in an Australia community: Prevalence, suicidal process, and help-seeking behavior. *Journal of Affective Disorders, 86,* 215–224.

Demos, J. (2008). *The enemy within: A short history of witch-hunting.* New York, NY: Penguin.

Dennett, D. C. (1993). *Consciousness explained.* Boston, MA: Little Brown & Co,

Dennis, M., & Reis, E. (2015). Women as witches. Witches as women: Witchcraft and patriarchy in colonial North America. In T. A. Foster (Ed.), *Women in early America* (pp. 66–94). New York, NY: New York University Press.

Derry, S. J. (1996). Cognitive schema theory in the constructivist debate. *Educational Psychologist, 31,* 163–174.

Dhadphale, M., & Shaikh, S. P. (1983). Epidemic hysteria in a Zambian school: "The mysterious madness of Mwinilunga". *British Journal of Psychiatry, 142,* 85–88.

Diamond, J. (2012). *The world until yesterday: What can we learn from traditional societies?* New York, NY: Viking.

Didi-Huberman, G. (2003). *Invention of hysteria: Charcot and the photographic icolography of the Salpêtrière.* Cambridge, MA: MIT Press. Originally published in 1982.

Diekstra, R. F. W. (1996). The epidemiology of suicide and parasuicide. *Archives of Suicide Research, 2,* 1–29.

Dijksterhuis, A. (2005). Why we are social animals: The high road to imitation as social glue. In S. Hurley & N. Chater (Eds.), *Perspectives on imitation: From neuroscience to social science. Volume 2: Imitation, human development, and culture* (pp. 207–220). Cambridge, MA: MIT Press.

Donald, M. (2005). Imitation and mimesis. In S. Hurley & N. Chater (Eds.), *Perspectives `on imitation: From neuroscience to social science. Volume 2: Imitation, human development,* and culture (pp. 283–300). Cambridge, MA: MIT Press.

Donne, J. (1982). *Biathanatos.* Ann Arbor, MI: ProQuest. Originally published in 1647.

Douglas, J. D. (1967). *The social meanings of suicide.* Princeton, NJ: Princeton University Press.

Dour, H. J., Cha, C. B., & Nock, M. K. (2011). Evidence for an emotion-cognition interaction in the statistical prediction of suicide attempts. *Behavior Research and Therapy, 49,* 294–298.

Droit, R.-P., & Sperber, D. (1999). *Des idées qui viennent.* Paris: Jacob.

Durkheim, E. (1951). *Suicide: A study in sociology* (pp. 41–53). New York, NY: Free Press. Originally published in 1897.

Durkheim, E. (1964 [1938]). *The rules of sociological method* (S. Solovay & J. H. Catlin, Trans.). New York, NY: The Free Press.

Durkheim, E. (1995 [1912]). *The elementary forms of religious life* (K. E. Fields, Trans.). New York, NY: The Free Press.

Echohawk, M. (1997). Suicide: The scourge of Native American people. *Suicide and Life-Threatening Behavior, 27,* 60–67.

Elliot, S. G. (1927). The diffusion of culture. In G. B. Malinowski, H. J. Spinden, & A. Goldweiser (Eds.), *Culture: The diffusion controversy* (pp. 9–25). New York, NY: Norton.

Ellis, T. E. (2006a). Epilogue: What have we learned about cognition and suicide and what more do we need to know? In T. E. Ellis (Ed.), *Cognition and suicide: Theory, research, and therapy* (pp. 369–380). Washington, DC: American Psychological Association.

Ellis, T. E. (2006b). The study of cognition and suicide: Beginnings and developmental milestones. In T. E. Ellis (Ed.), *Cognition and suicide: Theory, research, and therapy* (pp. 13–28). Washington, DC: American Psychological Association.

Ellis, T. E., & Cory, F. N. (1996). *Choosing to live: How to defeat suicide through cognitive therapy.* Oakland, CA: New Harbinger.

Ellis, T. E., & Ratliff, K. G. (1986). Cognitive characteristics of suicidal and nonsuicidal psychiatric inpatients. *Cognitive Therapy and Research, 10,* 625–634.

Ellis, T. E., & Rutherford, B. (2008). Cognition and suicide: Two decades of progress. *Journal of Cognitive Therapy, 1,* 47–68.

Erickson, P. A., & Murphy, L. D. (2013). *A history of anthropological theory* (4th ed.). Toronto, ON: University of Toronto Press.

Eriksen, T. H., & Nielsen, F. S. (2001). *A history of anthropology.* London, UK: Pluto.

Etzioni, A. (2000). Social norms: Internalization, persuasion, and history. *Law and Society Review, 34,* 157–178.

Evans, E., Hawton, K., Rodham, K., & Deeks, J. (2005). The prevalence of suicidal phenomena in adolescents: A systematic review of population-based studies. *Suicide and Life-Threatening Behavior, 35,* 239–250.

Evans, H., & Bartholomew, R. E. (2009). *Outbreak! The encyclopedia of extraordinary social behavior.* San Antonio, TX: Anomalist Books.

Exeter, D. J., & Boyle, P. J. (2007). Does young adult suicide cluster geographically in Scotland? *Journal of Epidemiology and Community Health, 61,* 731–736.

Eyman, J. R., & Kulick, E. (1996). An interpretation of Freud's ideas about suicide. In A. Leenaars & D. Lester (Eds.), *Suicide and the unconscious* (pp. 32–66). Northvale, NJ: Jason Aronson.

Fancher, R. E. (1973). *Psychoanalytic psychology: The development of Freud's thought.* Oxford, UK: Norton.

Farberow, N. L. (1975). Cultural history of suicide. In Norman L. F. (Ed.), *Suicide in different cultures* (pp. 1–15). Baltimore, MD: University Park Press.

Farberow, N. L., & Sheidman, S. S. (1961). *The cry for help*. New York, NY: McGraw-Hill.

Farr, R. M., & Serge M. (Eds.). (1984). *Social representations*. Cambridge, UK: Cambridge University Press.

Fast, J. A. (2017, May 19). Chris Cornell: When suicide doesn't make sense: What might have been happening inside the rock star's mind. *Psychology Today*.

Fenton, W. N. (1941). Iroquois suicide: A study in the stability of a culture pattern. *Bureau of American Ethnology Bulletin, 128*, 49–137.

Firth, R. (1961). Suicide and risk-taking in Tikopia society. *Psychiatry, 24*, 1–17.

Fivush, R., & Buckner, J. (1997). The self as socially constructed: A commentary. In U. Neisser & D. A. Jopling (Eds.), *The conceptual self in context: Culture. Experience, self-understanding* (pp. 176–181). New York, NY: Cambridge University Press.

Fleischer, J. (2011). *The latest craze: A short history of mass hysteria*. New York, NY: Fall River Press.

Frances, A. (2013). *Saving normal: An insider's revolt against out-of-control psychiatric diagnosis, DSM-5, big pharma, and the medicalization of ordinary life*. New York, NY: HarperCollins.

Freedman, J. L. (1982). Theories of contagion as they relate to mass psychogenic illness. In M. J. Colligan, J. W. Pennebaker, & L. R. Murphy (Eds.), *Mass psychogenic illness: A social psychological analysis* (pp. 171–182). Hillsdale, NJ: Lawrence Erlbaum.

Freeman, A., Reineke, M. A., & Beck, A. T. (1993). *Cognitive therapy of suicidal behavior: A manual for treatment*. New York, NY: Springer.

Freeman-Longo, R. E., & Blanchard, G. T. (1998). *Sexual abuse in America: Epidemic of the 21st century*. Brandon, VT: Safer Society Press.

Freud, S. (1917). Mourning and melancholia. In J. Strachey (Ed.), *Standard edition of the complete psychological works of Sigmund Freud* (Vol. 14, 237–258). New York, NY: Norton.

Fukurai, H., Butler, E. W., & Krooth, R. (1994). Sociologists in action: The McMartin sexual abuse case, litigation, justice, and mass hysteria. *The American Sociologist, 25*, 44–71.

Fullagar, S., & O-Brien, W. (2016). Speaking of suicide as a gendered problematic: Suicide attempts and recovery within women's narratives of depression. In J. White, I. Marsh, M. J. Kral, & J. Morris (Eds.), *Critical suicidology: Transforming suicide research and prevention for the 21st century* (pp. 94–112). Vancouver, BC: University of British Columbia Press.

Galasinski, D., & Ziolkowska, J. (2017). Construction of suicidal ideation in medical records. *Death Studies, 8*, 493–501.

Gale, D. (1996). What have we learned from social learning? *European Economic Review, 40*, 617–628.

Gardiner, H. W. (2001). Culture, context, and development. In D. Matsumoto (Ed.), *The handbook of culture and psychology* (pp. 101–118). New York, NY: Oxford University Press.

Garrels, S. R. (2011a). Human imitation: Historical, philosophical, and scientific perspectives. In S. R. Garrels (Ed.), *Mimesis and science: Empirical research on imitation and the mimetic theory of culture and religion* (pp. 1–38). East Lansing, MI: Michigan State University Press.

Garrels, S. R. (2011b). Mimesis and science: An interview with René Girard. In S. R. Garrels (Ed.), *Mimesis and science: Empirical research on imitation and the mimetic theory of culture and religion* (pp. 215–253). East Lansing, MI: Michigan State University Press.

Gebauer, G., & Wulf, C. (1995). *Mimesis: Culture, art, society.* Berkeley, CA: University of California Press.

Geertz, C. (1973). Think description: Toward an interpretive theory of culture. In C. Geertz (Ed.), *The interpretation of cultures.* New York, NY: Basic.

Geertz, C. (1983). *Local knowledge: Further essays in interpretive anthropology.* New York, NY: Basic.

Geertz, C. (1990). History and anthropology. *New Literary History, 21,* 321–335.

Gerber, J. J., & Macionis, L. M. (2010). *Sociology* (7th ed.). Toronto: Pearson Canada.

Gergen, K. J. (1999). *An invitation to social construction.* Thousand Oaks, CA: Sage.

Gergen, K. J. (2001). *Social construction in context.* Thousand Oaks, CA: Sage.

Gergen, K. J. (2010). Beyond the enlightenment: Relational being. In S. R. Kirschner & J. Martin (Eds.), *The sociocultural turn in psychology: The contextual emergence of mind and self* (pp. 68–87). New York, NY: Columbia University Press.

Gergen, K. J. (2011). *Relational being: Beyond self and community.* New York, NY: Oxford University Press.

Gibb, B. E., Andover, M. S., & Beach, S. R. H. (2006). Suicidal ideation and attitudes toward suicide. *Suicide and Life-Threatening Behavior, 36,* 12–18.

Gillham, J. E. (Ed.). (2000). *The science of optimism and hope: Research essays in honor of Martin E.P. Seligman.* Philadelphia, PA: Templeton Foundation Press.

Gilligan, J. (1996). *Violence: Reflections on a national epidemic.* New York, NY: Vintage Books.

Gladwell, M. (2000). *The tipping point: How little things can make a big difference.* Boston, MA: Little, Brown and Company.

Goeschel, C. (2009). *Suicide in Nazi Germany.* New York, NY: Oxford University Press.

Goldberg, M. J. (2014). *The myth of autism: How a misunderstood epidemic is destroying our children.* New York, NY: Skyhorse Publishing.

Good, B., & Kleinman, A. (1985). Epilogue: Culture and depression. In A. Kleinman & B. Good (Eds.), *Culture and depression: Studies in the anthropology and cross-cultural psychiatry of affect and disorder* (pp. 491–505). Berkeley, CA: University of California Press.

Goode, E. (2018, February 15). The things we know about school shooters. *The New York Times.*

Goodnow, J. J. (1990). The socialization of cognition: What's involved? In J. W. Stigler, R. A. Shweder, & G. Herdt (Eds.), *Cultural psychology: Essays on comparative human development* (pp. 259–286). New York, NY: Cambridge University Press.

Gordon, M. (1997). *Marshall McLuhan: Escape into understanding, a biography.* New York, NY: Basic.

Gould, M. S. (2001). Suicide and the media. *New York Academy of Sciences, 932,* 200–224.

Gould, M. S., Jamieson, P., & Romer, D. (2003). Media contagion and suicide among the young. *American Behavioral Scientist, 46,* 1269–1284.

Gould, M. S., & Shaffer, D. (1986). The impact of suicide in television movies. *The New England Journal of Medicine, 315,* 690–694.

Gould, M. S., Wallenstein, S., & Davidson, L. (1989). Suicide clusters: A critical review. *Suicide and Life-Threatening Behavior, 19,* 17–29.

Gould, S. J. (1981). *The mismeasure of man*. New York, NY: Norton.

Graeber, D. (2004). *Fragments of an anarchist anthropology*. Chicago, IL: Prickly Paradigm Press.

Graeber, D. (2007). *Possibilities: Essays on hierarchy, rebellion, and desire*. Oakland, CA: AK Press.

Grolnick, W. S., Deci, E. L., & Ryan, R. M. (1997). Internalization within the family: The self-determination theory perspective. In J. E. Grusec, & L. Kuczynski (Eds.), *Parenting and children's internalization of values: A handbook of contemporary theory* (pp. 135–161). New York, NY: Wiley.

Grosser, D., Polansky, N., & Lippittas, R. (1951). A laboratory study of behavioral contagion. *Human Relations, 4*, 115–142.

Gundach, J. H., & Stack, S. (1990). The impact of hyper media coverage on suicide: New York City, 1910–1920. *Social Science Quarterly, 71*, 619–628.

Hacking, I. (1999). *The social construction of what?* Cambridge, MA: Harvard University Press.

Hacking, I. (2002). *Mad travelers: Reflections on the reality of transient mental illnesses*. Cambridge, MA: Harvard University Press.

Hall, J. R. (1999). *Cultures of inquiry: From epistemology to discourse in sociohistorical research*. Cambridge, UK: Cambridge University Press.

Hanssens, L. (2007). The search to identify contagion operating within suicide clusters in Indigenous communities, Northern Territory, Australia. *Aboriginal and Islander Health Worker Journal, 31*, 27–33.

Harari, Y. N. (2011). *Sapiens: A brief history of humankind*. London, UK: Vintage.

Harper, D. W., & Voigt, L. (2007). Homicide followed by suicide: An integrated theoretical perspective. *Homicide Studies, 11*, 295–318.

Harris, M. (1974). *Cows, pigs, wars and witches: The riddles of culture*. New York, NY: Random House/Vintage.

Harris, M. (1999). *Theories of culture in postmodern times*. Walnut Creek, CA: AltaMira.

Hatfield, E., Cacioppo, J. T., & Rapson, R. L. (1994). *Emotional contagion: Studies in emotion and social interaction*. Cambridge, UK: Cambridge University Press.

Haw, C., Hawton, K., Niedzwiedz, C., & Platt, S. (2013). Suicide clusters: A review of risk factors and mechanisms. *Suicide and Life-Threatening Behavior, 43*, 97–108.

Hawton, K., Rodham, K., Evans, E., & Weatherall, R. (2002). Deliberate self harm in adolescents: Self report survey in schools in England. *British Medical Journal, 325*, 1207–1211.

Hays, J. N. (2005). *Epidemics and pandemics: Their impacts on human history*. Santa Barbara, CA: ABC-CLIO.

Hazell, P. (1993). Adolescent suicide clusters: Evidence, mechanisms and prevention. *Australian and New Zealand Journal of Psychiatry, 27*, 653–665.

Heath, C., & Heath, D. (2007). *Made to stick: Why some ideas take hold and others come unstuck*. London, UK: Random House.

Hebb, D. O. (1980). *Essay on mind*. Hillsdale, NJ: Lawrence Erlbaum Associates.

Hechter, M., & Opp, K.-D. (2001). What have we learned about the emergence of social norms? In M. Hechter & K. Opp (Eds.), *Social norms* (pp. 394–415). New York, NY: Russell Sage Foundation.

Heeringgen, K. V. (2012). Stress-diathesis model of suicidal behavior. In Y. Dwivedi (Ed.), *The neurobiological basis of suicide* (pp. 113–124). New York, NY: Taylor & Francis.

Hempel, J. (2014, August 22). Contagion: How the "selfie" became a social epidemic. *Fortune*.

Hendin, H. (1991). Psychodynamics of suicide, with particular reference to the young. *American Journal of Psychiatry*, *148*, 1150–1159.

Henrich, J. (2001). Cultural transmission and the diffusion of innovations: Adoption dynamics that biased cultural transmission is the predominate force in behavioral change. *American Anthropologist*, *103*, 992–1013.

Herzfeld, M. (2001). *Anthropology: Theoretical practice in culture and society*. Oxford, UK: Blackwell.

Herzog, H. (2006). Forty-two thousand and one Dalmatians: Fads, social contagion, and dog breed popularity. *Society and Animals*, *14*, 383–397.

Hess, U., & Blairy, S. (2001). Facial mimicry and emotional contagion to dynamic emotional facial expressions and their influence on decoding accuracy. *International Journal of Psychophysiology*, *40*, 129–141.

Hillman, J. (1964). *Suicide and the soul*. New York, NY: Harper & Row.

Hjelmeland, H. (2016). A critical look at current suicide research. In J. White, I. Marsh, M. J. Kral, & J. Morris (Eds.), *Critical suicidology: Transforming suicide research and prevention for the 21st century* (pp. 31–55). Vancouver, BC: University of British Columbia Press.

Hjelmeland, H., & Knizek, B. L. (2010). Why we need qualitative research in suicidology. *Suicide and Life-Threatening Behavior*, *40*, 74–80.

Hjelmeland, H., & Knizek, B. L. (2017). Suicide and mental disorders: A discourse of politics, power, and vested interests. *Death Studies*, *8*, 481–492.

Hjelmeland, H., & Knizek, B. L. (2019). The emperor's new clothes? A critical look at the interpersonal theory of suicide. *Death Studies*, online prepublication copy.

Hoffman, F. W., & Bailey, W. G. (1992). *Mind and society fads*. New York, NY: The Haworth Press.

Holden, R. R., Mehta, K., Cunningham, E. J., & Lindsay, L. D. (2001). Development and preliminary validation of a scale of psychache. *Canadian Journal of Behavioral Science*, *33*, 224–232.

Holland, D., & Naomi, Q. (1987). *Cultural models in language and thought*. Cambridge, UK: Cambridge University Press.

Honkasalo, M.-L., & Tuominen, M. (2014). *Culture, suicide and the human condition*. New York, NY: Berghahn.

Hopper, K., Harrison, G., & Wanderling, J. A. (2007). An overview of course and outcome in ISoS. In K. Hopper, G. Harrison, A. Janca, & N. Sartorius (Eds.), *Recovery from schizophrenia: An international perspective* (pp. 23–38). New York, NY: Oxford University Press.

Hopper, K., & Wanderling, J. (2000). Revisiting the developed versus developing country distinction in course and outcome in schizophrenia: Results from ISoS, the WHO collaborative followup project. *Schizophrenia Bulletin*, *26*, 835–846.

Horowitz, M. J., & Stinson, C. H. (1995). Defenses as aspects of person schemas and control processes. In H. R. Conte & R. Plutchik (Eds.), *Ego defenses: Theory and measurement* (pp. 79–97). New York, NY: Wiley.

Horwitz, A. V. (2002). *Creating mental illness*. Chicago, IL: University of Chicago Press.

Huh, G. Y., Jo, G. R., Kim, K. H., Ahn, Y. W., & Lee, S. Y. (2009). Imitative suicide by burning charcoal in the southeastern region of Korea: The influence of mass media reporting. *Legal Medicine, 11*, 563–564.

Hurley, S., & Chater, N. (Eds.). (2005a). *Perspectives on imitation: From neuroscience to social science. Volume 2: Imitation, human development, and culture*. Cambridge, MA: MIT Press.

Hurley, S., & Chater, N. (2005b). Introduction: The importance of imitation. In S. Hurley & N. Chater (Eds.), *Perspectives on imitation: From neuroscience to social science. Volume 1: Mechanisms of imitation and imitation in animals* (pp. 1–52). Cambridge, MA: MIT Press.

Hutchins, E. (1996). *Cognition in the wild*. Cambridge, MA: The MIT Press.

Hyman, S., & George, W. A. (1989). Suicide and affective disorders. In D. Jacobs & H. N. Brown (Eds.), *Suicide: Understanding and responding* (pp. 171–181). Madison, CT: International Universities Press.

Iacoboni, M. (2005). Understanding others: Imitation, language, and empathy. In S. Hurley & N. Chater (Eds.), *Perspectives on imitation: From neuroscience to social science. Volume 1: Mechanisms of imitation and imitation in animals* (pp. 77–99). Cambridge, MA: MIT Press.

Iacoboni, M., Woods, R. P., Brass, M., Bekkering, H., Mazziotta, J. C., & Rizzolatti, G. (1999). Cortical mechanisms of human imitation. *Science, 286*, 2526–2528.

Iyengar, R., Bulte, V., & Valente, T. W. (2011). Opinion leadership and social contagion in new product diffusion. *Marketing Science, 30*, 195–212.

Jackson, D. D. (1957). Theories of suicide. In E. S. Shneiedman & N. L. Farberow (Eds.), *Clues to suicide* (pp. 11–21). New York, NY: McGraw-Hill.

Jager-Hyman, S., Cunningham, A., Wenzel, A., Mattei, S., Brown, G. K., & Beck, A. T. (2014). Cognitive distortions and suicide attempts. *Cognitive Therapy and Research, 38*, 369–374.

James, W. (1904). *The principles of psychology*. New York, NY: Henry Holt and Company. Originally published 1890.

Jamison, K. R. (1999). *Night falls fast: Understanding suicide*. New York, NY: Knopf.

Janis, I. L. (1972). *Victims of groupthink*. Boston, MA: Houghton Mifflin.

Janney, J. E. (1941). Fad and fashion leadership among undergraduate women. *Journal of Abnormal and Social Psychology, 36*, 275–278.

Jaworski, K. (2014). *The gender of suicide: Knowledge production, theory and suicidology*. Burlington, VT: Ashgate.

Jaworski, K., & Scott, D. G. (2016). Understanding the unfathomable in suicide: Poetry, absence, and the corporeal body. In J. White, I. Marsh, M. J. Kral, & J. Morris (Eds.), *Critical suicidology: Transforming suicide research and prevention for the 21st century*. Vancouver, BC: University of British Columbia Press.

Jenkins, J. H. (1994). The psychocultural study of emotion and mental disorder. In P. K. Bock (Ed.), *Psychological anthropology* (pp. 97–120). Westport, CT: Praeger.

Jobes, D. A. (2003). Understanding suicide in the 21st century. *Preventing Suicide, 2*, 2–4.

Joe, S., Romer, D., & Jamieson, P. E. (2007). Suicide acceptability is related to suicide planning in U.S. adolescents and young adults. *Suicide and Life-Threatening Behavior, 37*, 165–178.

Joiner, T. E. (2005). *Why people die by suicide*. Cambridge, MA: Harvard University Press.

Joiner, T. E., Hom, M. A., Hagan, C. R., & Silva, C. (2016). Suicide as a derangement of the self-sacrificial aspect of eusociality. *Psychological Review, 123*, 235–254.

Jollant, F., Bellivier, F., Leboyer, M., Astruc, B., Torres, S., Verdier, R., . . . & Courtet, P. (2005). Impaired decision making in suicide attempters. *The American Journal of Psychiatry, 162*, 304–310.

Jones, K. (1991). The culture of the mental hospital. In G. E. Berrios & H. Freeman (Eds.), *150 years of British psychiatry, 1841–1991* (pp. 17–28). London, UK: Gaskell.

Jones, R. A. (2001 [1997]). The *other* Durkheim: History and theory in the treatment of classical sociological thought. In W. S. F. Pickering (Ed.), *Emile Durkheim: Critical assessments of leading sociologists* (Vol. 1, pp. 313–339). London, UK: Routledge.

Jones, S. S. (2007). Imitation in infancy: The development of mimicry. *Psychological Science, 18*, 593–599.

Kagan, J. (1998). *Three seductive ideas*. Cambridge, MA: Harvard University Press.

Kahneman, D. (2011). *Thinking, fast and slow*. New York, NY: Penguin.

Kalesan, B., Villarreal, M. D., Keyes, K. M., & Galea, S. (2016). Gun ownership and social gun culture. *Injury Prevention, 22*, 125–135.

Karsenti, B. (2010). Imitation: Returning to the Tarde-Durkheim debate. In M. Candea (Ed.), *The social after Gabriel Tarde: Debates and assessments* (pp. 44–61). New York, NY: Routledge.

Kashima, Y. (2001). Culture and social cognition: Toward a social psychology of cultural dynamics. In D. Matsumoto (Ed.), *The handbook of culture and psychology* (pp. 325–360). New York, NY: Oxford University Press.

Katz, E. (2006). Rediscovering Gabriel Tarde. *Political Communication, 3*, 263–270.

Kaufman, J., & Patterson, O. (2005). Cross-national cultural diffusion: The global spread of cricket. *American Sociological Review, 70*, 82–110.

Keller, J. D. (1992). Schemes for schemata. In T. Schwartz, G. M. White, & C. A. Lutz (Eds.), *New directions in psychological anthropology* (pp. 59–67). New York, NY: Cambridge University Press.

Kellerman, A. L., Rivara, F. P., Somes, G., Reay, D. T., Francisco, J., Banton, J. G., . . . & Hackman, B. B. (1992). Suicide in the home in relation to gun ownership. *New England Journal of Medicine, 327*, 467–472.

Kerckoff, A. C. (1982). A social psychological view of mass psychogenic illness. In M. J. Colligan, J. W. Pennebaker, & L. R. Murphy (Eds.), *Mass psychogenic illness: A social psychological analysis* (pp. 199–215). Hillsdale, NJ: Lawrence Erlbaum.

Kerckoff, A. C., & Back, K. W. (1968). *The June bug: A study of hysterical contagion*. New York, NY: Appleton-Century-Crofts.

Khan, M. M. (1998). Suicide and attempted suicide in Pakistan. *Crisis, 19*, 172–176.

Killias, M. (1993). International correlations between gun ownership and rates of homicide and suicide. *Canadian Medical Association Journal, 148,* 1721–1725.

Kinnunen, J. (1996). Gabriel Tarde as a founding father of innovation diffusion research. *Acta Sociologica, 39,* 431–442.

Kirmayer, L. J. (1994). Suicide among Canadian Aboriginal peoples. *Transcultural Psychiatry, 31,* 91–110.

Kirmayer, L. J., Fletcher, C., & Boothroyd, L. J. (1998). Suicide among the Inuit of Canada. In A. A. Leenaars, S. Wenckstern, I. Sakinofsky, R. Dyck, M. J. Kral, & R. Bland (Eds.), *Suicide in Canada* (pp. 189–211). Toronto, ON: University of Toronto Press.

Kirshner, D., & James, A. W. (Eds.). (1997). *Situated cognition: Social, semiotic, and psychological perspectives.* Mahwah, NJ: Lawrence Erlbaum.

Kitayama, S., Duffy, S., & Uchida, Y. (2007). Self as a cultural mode of being. In S. Kitayama & D. Cohen (Eds.), *Handbook of cultural psychology* (pp. 136–174). New York, NY: Guilford.

Kitayama, S., & Uskul, A. K. (2011). Culture, mind, and the brain: Current evidence and future directions. *Annual Review of Psychology, 62,* 419–449.

Kleinman, A. Veena, D., & Margaret, L. (Eds.). (1997). *Social suffering.* Berkeley, CA: University of California Press.

Kodres, L. E., & Pritsker, M. (2002). A rational expectations model of financial contagion. *The Journal of Finance, 57,* 769–799.

Köhler, W. (1927). *The mentality of apes.* New York, NY: Harcourt, Brace.

Kokota, D. (2011). View point: Episodes of mass hysteria in African schools: A study of literature. *Malawi Medical Journal, 23,* 74–77.

Kposowa, A. J. (2013). Association of suicide rates, gun ownership, conservatism, and individual suicide risk. *Social Psychiatry and Psychiatric Epidemiology, 48,* 1467–1479.

Kral, M. J. (1994). Suicide as social logic. *Suicide and Life-Threatening Behavior, 24,* 245–255.

Kral, M. J. (1998). Suicide and the internalization of culture: Three questions. *Cultural Psychiatry, 35,* 221–233.

Kral, M. J. (2012). Postcolonial suicide among Inuit in Arctic Canada. *Culture, Medicine and Psychiatry, 36,* 306–325.

Kral, M. J. (2013). "The weight on our shoulders is too much, and we are falling": Suicide among Inuit male youth in Nunavut, Canada. *Medical Anthropology Quarterly, 27,* 63–83.

Kral, M. J. (in press). *The return of the sun: Suicide and reclamation among Inuit in Arctic Canada.* New York, NY: Oxford University Press.

Kral, M. J., & Idlout, L. (2016). Indigenous best practices: Community-based suicide prevention in Nunavut, Canada. In J. White, I. Marsh, M. J. Kral, & J. Morris (Eds.), *Critical suicidology: Transforming suicide research and prevention for the 21st century* (pp. 229–243). Vancouver, BC: University of British Columbia Press.

Kral, M. J., & Johnson, E. A. (1996). Suicide, self-deception, and the cognitive unconscious. In A. A. Leenaars & D. Lester (Eds.), *Suicide and the unconscious* (pp. 67–89). Northvale, NJ: Jason Aronson.

Kral, M. J., & Walsh, S. J. (2000). The cultural geography of suicide in the Canadian Arctic. In J. L. McIntosh (Ed.), *Suicide 2000: Proceedings of the 33rd annual conference of the American Association of Suicidology.* Washington, DC: American Association of Suicidology.

Kral, M. J., & White, J. (Eds.). (2017). Special issue on critical suicidology. *Death Studies, 8,* 469–471.

Kral, M. J., Wiebe, P., Nisbet, K., Dallas, C., Okalik, L., Enuaraq, N., & Cinotta, J. (2009). Canadian Inuit community engagement in suicide prevention. *International Journal of Circumpolar Health, 68,* 91–107.

Krieger, G. (1974). The plasma level of cortisol as a predictor of suicide. *Diseases of the Nervous System, 35,* 237–240.

Kroeber, A. L. (1940). Stimulus diffusion. *American Anthropologist, 42,* 1–20.

Kroeber, A. L., & Clyde, K. (1963 [1952]). *Culture: A critical review of concepts and definitions.* New York, NY: Vintage.

Kuhn, T. S. (1977). *The essential tension.* Chicago, IL: University of Chicago Press.

Kuklick, H. (1996). Diffusionism. In A. Barnard & J. Spencer (Eds.), *Encyclopedia of social and cultural anthropology* (pp. 160–162). London, UK: Routledge.

Kuper, A. (2000). If memes are the answer, what is the question? In R. Aunger (Ed.), *Darwinizing culture: The status of memetics as a science* (pp. 189–203). Oxford, UK: Oxford University Press.

Kushner, H. I. (1989). *Self-destruction in the promised land: A psychocultural biology of American suicide.* New Brunswick, NJ: Rutgers University Press.

Kushner, H. I., & Sterk, C. E. (2005). The limits of social capital: Durkheim, suicide, and social cohesion. *American Journal of Public Health, 95,* 1139–1143.

LaCapra, D. (2001). *Emile Durkheim: Sociologist and philosopher* (rev. ed.). Aurora, CO: The Davies Group.

La Fontaine, J. (1975). Anthropology. In S. Perlin (Ed.), *A handbook for the study of suicide* (pp. 77–91). New York, NY: Oxford University Press.

Laird, H. A. (2011). Between the (disciplinary) acts: Modernist suicidology. *Modernism/Modernity, 18,* 525–550.

Lambert, M. T., & Silva, P. S. (1998). An update on the impact of gun control legislation on suicide. *Psychiatric Quarterly, 69,* 127–134.

Lasaga, J. I. (1980). Death in Jonestown: Techniques of political control by a paranoid leader. *Suicide and Life-Threatening Behavior, 10,* 210–216.

Latour, B. (2002). Gabriel Tarde and the end of the social. In P. Joyce (Ed.), *The social in question: New bearings in history and the social sciences* (pp. 117–132). London, UK: Routledge.

Latour, B. (2010). Tarde's idea of quantification. In M. Candea (Ed.), *The social after Gabriel Tarde: Debates and assessments* (pp. 145–162). London, UK: Routledge.

Laugrand, F. B., & Oosten, J. G. (2010). *Inuit Shamanism and Christianity: Transitions and transformations in the twentieth century.* Montreal, QC & Kingston, ON: McGill-Queen's University Press.

Law, C., Sveticic, J., & De Leo, D. (2014). Restricting access to a suicide hotspot does not shift the problem to another location: An experiment of two river bridges in Brisbane, Australia. *Australian and New Zealand Journal of Public Health, 38,* 134–138.

Lawrence, J. A., & Valsiner, J. (1993). Conceptual roots of internalization: From transmission to transformation. *Human Development, 36,* 150–167.

Layton, R. (1997). *An introduction to theory in anthropology.* Cambridge, UK: Cambridge University Press.

Le Bon, G. (1960). *The crowd.* New York, NY: Taylor & Francis. Originally published 1895.

Leach, M. M. (2006). *Cultural diversity and suicide: Ethnic, religious, gender, and sexual orientation perspectives.* New York, NY: Hawthorn Press.

Leach, M. M., & Leong, F. T. L. (2008). Challenges for research on suicide among ethnic minorities. In F. T. L. Leong & M. M. Leach (Eds.), *Suicide among racial and ethnic minority groups: Theory, research, and practice* (pp. 297–318). New York, NY: Routledge.

Lee, J., Hwang, J.-S., & Stack, S. J. (2014). To what extent does the reporting behavior of the media regarding a celebrity suicide influence subsequent suicides in South Korea? *Suicide and Life-Threatening Behavior, 44,* 457–472.

Leenaars, A. A., Moksony, F., Lester, D., & Wenckstern, S. (2010). The impact of gun control (Bill C-51) on suicide in Canada. *Death Studies, 27,* 103–124.

Leong, F. T. L., & Leach, M. M. (Eds.). (2008). *Suicide among racial and ethnic minority groups: Theory, research, and practice.* New York, NY: Routledge.

Leont'ev, A. N. (1981). The problem of activity in psychology. In J. V. Wertsch (Ed.), *The concept of activity in Soviet psychology* (pp. 37–71). New York, NY: M. E. Sharpe Inc.

Lerner, M. S., & Clum, G. A. (1990). Treatment of suicidal ideators: A problem-solving approach. *Behavior Therapy, 21,* 403–411.

Lester, D. (1988). Research note gun control, gun ownership, and suicide prevention. *Suicide and Life-Threatening Behavior, 18,* 176–180.

Lester, D. (1996a). Jungian perspectives on the unconscious and suicide. In A. Leenaars & D. Lester (Eds.), *Suicide and the unconscious* (pp. 49–66). Northvale, NJ: Jason Aronson.

Lester, D. (1996b). *Patterns of suicide and homicide in the world.* Commack, NY: Nova Science.

Lester, D. (2008). Theories of suicide. In F. T. Leong & M. M. Leach (Eds.), *Suicide among racial and ethnic minority groups: Theory, research, and practice* (pp. 39–53). New York, NY: Routledge.

Lester, D. (2013). Suicide and culture. In D. Lester & J. R. Rogers (Eds.), *Understanding suicide: A global issue* (pp. 209–232). Santa Barbara, CA: Praeger.

Lester, D., & Stack, S. (2015). Conclusion. In D. Lester & S. Stack (Eds.), *Suicide as a dramatic performance.* New Brunswick, NJ: Transaction Publishers.

Lester, D., Stack, S., Schmidke, A., Schaller, S., & Muller, I. (2005). Mass homicide and suicide. *Crisis, 26,* 184–187.

LeVine, R. A. (1973). *Culture, behavior, and personality.* Chicago, IL: Aldine.

Levy, D. A., & Nail, P. R. (1993). Contagion: A theoretical and empirical review and reconceptualization. *Genetic, Social, and General Psychology Monographs, 119,* 233–284.

Lewis, M. (1997). *Altering fate: Why the past does not predict the future.* New York, NY: Guilford.

Li, X., Xiao, Z., & Xiao, S. (2009). Suicide among the elderly in mainland China. *Psychogeriatrics, 9,* 62–66.

Lindholm, C. (2007). *Culture and identity: The history, theory, and practice of psychological anthropology* (2nd ed.). Boston, MA: McGraw Hill.

Linehan, M. M., Armstrong, H. E., Suarez, A., Allmon, D., & Heard, H. L. (1991). Cognitive-behavioral treatment of chronically parasuicidal borderline patients. *Archives of General Psychiatry, 48,* 1060–1064.

Litman, R. E. (1967). Sigmund Freud on suicide. In E. S. Shneidman (Ed.), *Essays in self-destruction* (pp. 324–344). New York, NY: Science House, Inc.

Liu, K. Y., Beautrais, A., Caine, E., Chan, K., Chao, A., Conwell, Y., . . . & Yip, P. (2007). Charcoal burning suicides in Hong Kong and urban Taiwan: An illustration of the impact of a novel suicide method on overall regional rates. *Journal of Epidemiology and Community Health*, 61, 248–253.

Liu, R. X. (2006). Vulnerability to friends' suicidal influence: The moderating effects of gender and adolescent depression. *Journal of Youth and Adolescence*, 35, 479–489.

Lubin, G., Werbeloff, N., Halperin, D., Shmushkevitch, M., Weiser, M., & Knobler, H. Y. (2010). Decrease in suicide rates after a change of policy reducing access to firearms in adolescents: A naturalistic epidemiological study. *Suicide and Life-Threatening Behavior*, 40, 421–424.

Lukes, S. (1973). *Emile Durkheim: His life and work, a historical and critical study*. Stanford, CA: Stanford University Press.

Lutz, C. A. (1988). *Unnatural emotions: Everyday sentiments on a Micronesian atoll and their challenge to Western theory*. Chicago, IL: University of Chicago Press.

MacDonald, M. (1989). The medicalization of suicide in England: Laymen, physicians, and cultural change, 1500–1870. *The Milbank Quarterly*, 67(Suppl. 1), 69–91.

Mackay, C. (1852). *Memoirs of extraordinary popular delusions and the madness of crowds* (2nd ed.). London, UK: Office of the National Illustrated Library.

Mahar, C., Harker, R., & Wilkes, C. (1990). The basic theoretical position. In R. Harker, C. Mahar, & C. Wilkes (Eds.), *An introduction to the work of Pierre Bourdieu: The practice of theory* (pp. 1–25). London, UK: MacMillan.

Malinowski, B. (1932). *Argonauts of the western pacific*. London, UK: George Routledge & Sons, Ltd.

Maltsberger, J. T. (1999). The psychodynamic understanding of suicide. In D. G. Jacobs (Ed.), *The Harvard Medical School guide to suicide assessment and intervention* (pp. 72–82). San Francisco, CA: Jossey-Bass.

Maltsberger, J. T., & Mark, J. G. (Eds.). (1996). *Essential papers on suicide*. New York, NY: New York University Press.

Mancinelli, I., Comparelli, A., Girardi, P., & Tatarelli, R. (2002). Mass suicide: Historical and psychodynamic considerations. *Suicide and Life-Threatening Behavior*, 32, 91–100.

Marcovitz, H. (2018). *The opioid epidemic*. San Diego, CA: ReferencePoint Press.

Maris, R. W. (1992). How are suicides different? In R. W. Maris, A. L. Berman, J. T. Maltsberger, & R. Yufit (Eds.), *Pathways to suicide: A survey of self-destructive behaviors* (pp. 65–87). New York, NY: Guilford.

Markus, H. R., & Hamedani, M. G. (2007). Sociocultural psychology: The dynamic interdependence among self systems and social systems. In S. Kitayama & D. Cohen (Eds.), *Handbook of cultural psychology* (pp. 3–39). New York, NY: Guilford.

Markus, H. R., Mullally, P. R., & Kitayama, S. (1997). Selfways: Diversity in modes of cultural participation. In U. Neisser & D. A. Jopling (Eds.), *The conceptual self in context: Culture, experience, self-understanding* (pp. 13–61). New York, NY: Cambridge University Press.

Marsella, A. J., Sartorius, N., Jablensky, A., & Fenton, F. R. (1985). Cross-cultural studies of depressive disorders: An overview. In A. Kleinman & B. Good (Eds.), *Culture and depression: Studies in the anthropology and cross-cultural psychiatry of affect and disorder* (pp. 299–324). Berkeley, CA: University of California Press.

Marsella, A. J., & Yamada, A. M. (2007). Culture and psychopathology: Foundations, issues, and directions. In S. Kitayama & D. Cohen (Eds.), *Handbook of cultural psychology* (pp. 797–820). New York, NY: Guilford.

Marsh, I. (2010). *Suicide: Foucault, history and truth*. Cambridge, UK: Cambridge University Press.

Marsh, I. (2016). Critiquing contemporary suicidology. In J. White, I. Marsh, M. J. Kral, & J. Morris (Eds.), *Critical suicidology: Transforming suicide research and prevention for the 21st century* (pp. 15–30). Vancouver, BC: University of British Columbia Press.

Martin, J., & Sugarman, J. (1999). *The psychology of human possibility and constraint*. Albany, NY: State University of New York Press.

Martin, J., & Sugarman, J. (2003). A theory of personhood for psychology. In D. B. Hill & M. J. Kral (Eds.), *About psychology: Essays at the crossroads of history, theory, and philosophy* (pp. 73–87). Albany, NY: State University of New York Press.

Martin, J., Sugarman, J., & Thompson, J. (2003). *Psychology and the question of agency*. Albany, NY: State University of New York Press.

Martinez, J. (2015). Suicide and the communicative condition: Audience and the idea of suicide. In D. Lester & S. Stack (Eds.), *Suicide as a dramatic performance* (pp. 51–72). New Brunswick, NJ: Transaction Publishers.

Marzuk, P. M., Tardiff, K., & Hirsch, C. S. (1992). The epidemiology of murder-suicide. *Journal of the American Medical Association, 267*, 3179–3183.

Mattingly, C., Lutkehaus, N. C., & Throop, C. J. (2008). Bruner's search for meaning: A conversation between psychology and anthropology. *Ethos, 36*, 1–28.

Mattoo, S. K., Gupta, N., Lobana, A., & Bedi, B. (2002). Mass family hysteria: A report from India. *Psychiatry and Clinical Neurosciences, 56*, 643–646.

May, P. A., Van Winkle, N. W., Williams, M. B., McFeeley, P. J., DeBruyn, L. M., & Serna, P. (2002). Alcohol and suicide death among American Indians of New Mexico: 1980–1998. *Suicide and Life-Threatening Behavior, 32*, 240–255.

McCauley, C. (1989). The nature of social influence in groupthink: Compliance and internalization. *Journal of Personality and Social Psychology, 57*, 250–260.

McIntosh, J. L., & Santos, J. F. (1982). Changing patterns in methods of suicide by race and sex. *Suicide and Life-Threatening Behavior, 12*, 221–233.

McKenzie, N., & Keane, M. (2007). Contributions of imitative suicide to the suicide rate in prisons. *Suicide and Life-Threatening Behavior, 37*, 538–542.

Mead, M. (1972). *Blackberry winter: My earlier years*. Gloucester, MA: Peter Smith.

Meltzer, H., & Lowy, M. (1989). The neuroendocrine system and suicide. In L. Davidson & M. Linnoila (Eds.), *Report of the Secretary's Task Force on youth suicide* (pp. 235–246). Washington, DC: U.S. Government Printing Office.

Meltzoff, A. N. (2005). Imitation and other minds: The "like me" hypothesis. In S. Hurley & N. Chater (Eds.), *Perspectives on imitation: From neuroscience to social science. Volume 2: Imitation, human development, and culture* (pp. 55–77). Cambridge, MA: MIT Press.

Meltzoff, A. N. (2011). Out of the mouths of babes: Imitation, gaze, and intentions in infant research: The "like me" framework. In S. R. Garrels (Ed.), *Mimesis and science: Empirical research on imitation and the mimetic theory of culture and religion* (pp. 55–74). East Lansing, MI: Michigan State University Press.

Meltzoff, A. N., & Moore, M. K. (1977). Imitation of facial and manual gestures by human neonates. *Science, 4312*, 75–78.

Meltzoff, A. N., & Moore, M. K. (1983). Newborn infants imitate adult facial gestures. *Child Development, 54*, 702–779.

Menninger, K. A. (1933). Psychoanalytic aspects of suicide. *International Journal of Psychoanalysis, 14*, 376–390.

Menninger, K. A. (1938). *Man against himself.* New York, NY: Harcourt Brace.

Mesquita, B., & Leu, J. (2007). The cultural psychology of emotion. In S. Kitayama & D. Cohen (Eds.), *Handbook of cultural psychology* (pp. 734–759). New York, NY: Guilford.

Mestrovic, S. G. (1992). *Durkheim and postmodern culture.* New York, NY: Aldine de Gruyter.

Meyersohn, R., & Katz, E. (1957). Notes on the natural history of fads. *American Journal of Sociology, 62*, 594–601.

Micale, M. S. (1989). Hysteria and its historiography: A review of past and present writings (I). *History of Science, 27*, 223–261.

Micale, M. S. (1995). *Approaching hysteria: Disease and its interpretations.* Princeton, NJ: Princeton University Press.

Miller, J. G. (2007). Cultural psychology of moral development. In S. Kitayama & D. Cohen (Eds.), *Handbook of cultural psychology* (pp. 477–499). New York, NY: Guilford.

Miller, M., Azrael, D., & Hemenway, D. (2002). Household firearm ownership and suicide rates in the United States. *Epidemiology, 13*, 517–524.

Miller, M., Lippmann, S. J., Azrael, D., & Hemenway, D. (2007). Household firearm ownership and rates of suicide across the 50 United States. *Journal of Trauma and Acute Care Surgery, 62*, 1029–1035.

Miller, N., & Dollard, J. (1941). *Social learning and imitation.* New Haven, CT: Yale University Press.

Milloy, J. S. & McCallum, M. J. L. (1999). *A national crime: The Canadian government and the residential school system.* Winnipeg, MB: University of Manitoba Press.

Minkoff, K., Bergman, E., Beck, A. T., & Beck, R. (2006). Hopelessness, depression, and attempted suicide. *American Journal of Psychiatry, 130*, 455–459.

Minois, G. (1999). *History of suicide: Voluntary death in Western culture* (L. G. Cochrane, Trans.). Baltimore, MD: John Hopkins University Press.

Miscellany. (1845). Napoleon's order against suicide. *American Journal of Insanity, 2*, 93.

Moffatt, M. E. K. (1982). Epidemic hysteria in a Montreal train station. *Pediatrics, 70*, 308–310.

Morgenroth, T., Ryan, M. K., & Peters, K. (2015). The motivational theory of role modeling: How role models influence role aspirants' goals. *Review of General Psychology, 19*, 465–483.

Morling, B., & Kitayama, S. (2008). Culture and motivation. In J. Y. Shah & W. L. Gardner (Eds.), *Handbook of motivation science* (pp. 417–433). New York, NY: Guilford.

Morris, J. (2016). Risky bodies: Making suicide knowable among youth. In J. White, I. Marsh, M. J. Kral, & J. Morris (Eds.), *Critical suicidology: Transforming suicide research and prevention for the 21st century* (pp. 71–93). Vancouver, BC: University of British Columbia Press.

Morselli, H. (1882). *Suicide: An essay on comparative moral statistics*. New York, NY: D. Appleton and Company.

Mościcki, E. K. (1997). Identification of suicide risk factors using epidemiologic studies. *Psychiatric Clinics of North America, 20*, 499–517.

Moscovici, S. (1981). On social representations. In J. P. Forgas (Ed.), *Social cognition: Perspectives on everyday understanding* (pp. 181–209). New York, NY: Academic Press.

Motto, J. A. (1992). An integrated approach to estimating suicide risk. In R. W. Maris, A. L. Berman, J. T. Maltsberger, & R. I. Yufit (Eds.), *Assessment and prediction of suicide* (pp. 625–639). New York, NY: Guilford.

Motto, J. A. (1993). Looking back. In A. A. Leenaars (Ed.), *Suicidology: Essays in honor of Edwin Shneidman* (pp. 22–34). Northvale, NJ: Jason Aronson.

Mueller, A. S., & Arbutyn, S. (2014). Can social ties be harmful? Examining the spread of suicide is early adulthood. *Sociological Perspectives, 58*, 204–222.

Mueller, A. S., & Abrutyn, S. (2016). Adolescents under pressure: A new Durkheimian framework for understanding adolescent suicide in a cohesive community. *American Sociological Review, 51*, 877–899.

Mueller, A. S., Abrutyn, S., & Stockton, C. (2015). Can social ties be harmful? Examining the social dynamics of suicide suggestion in early adulthood. *Sociological Perspectives, 58*, 38–45.

Mueller, A. S., Abrutyn, S., & Stockton, C. (in press). Can social ties be harmful? Examining the spread of suicide in early adulthood. *Sociological Perspectives, 58*, 204–222.

Munro, D., Schumaker, J. F., & Carr, S. C. (1997). *Motivation and culture*. New York, NY: Routledge.

Münster, D., & Broz, L. (2015). The anthropology of suicide: Ethnography and the tension of agency. In L. Broz & D. Münster (Eds.), *Suicide and agency: Anthropological perspectives on self-destruction, personhood, and power*. Farnham: Ashgate.

Murray, H. A., & Kluckhohn, C. (1953). Outline of a conception of personality. In C. Kluckhohn & H. A. Murray (Eds.), *Personality in nature, society, and culture* (pp. 3–49). New York, NY: Alfred A. Knopf.

Nadel, J., & Butterworth, G. (Eds.). (1999). *Imitation in infancy*. Cambridge, UK: Cambridge University Press.

Nakalawa, L., Musisi, S., Kinyanda, E., & Okello, E. S. (2010). Demon attack disease: A case report of mass hysteria after mass trauma in a primary school in Uganda. *African Journal of Traumatic Stress, 1*, 43–53.

Nehaniv, C. L., & Dautenhahn, K. (Eds.). (2007). *Imitation and social learning in robots, humans and animals: Behavioral, social and communicative dimensions*. Cambridge, UK: Cambridge University Press.

Neumann, R., & Strack, F. (2000). "Mood contagion": The automatic transfer of mood between persons. *Journal of Personality and Social Psychology, 79*, 211–223.

Neuringer, C. (1961). Dichotomous evaluations in suicidal individuals. *Journal of Consulting Psychology, 25*, 445–449.

Neuringer, C. (1964). Rigid thinking in suicidal individuals. *Journal of Consulting Psychology, 28*, 54–58.

Neuringer, C., & Lettieri, D. J. (1971). Cognition, attitude, and affect in suicidal individuals. *Suicide and Life-Threatening Behavior, 1*, 106–112.

Nichter, M. (1981). Idioms of distress: Alternatives in the expression of psychosocial distress: A case study from South India. *Culture, Medicine, and Psychiatry,* 5, 379–408.

Nichter, M. (2010). Idioms of distress revisited. *Culture, Medicine, and Psychiatry, 34,* 401–416.

Niederkrotenthaler, T., Till, B., Kapusta, N. D., Voracek, M., Dervic, K., & Sonneck, G. (2009). Copycat effects after media reports on suicide: A population-based ecologic study. *Social Science and Medicine, 69,* 1085–1090.

Niedzwiedz, C., Haw, C., Hawton, K., & Platt, S. (2014). The definition and epidemiology of clusters of suicidal behavior: A systematic review. *Suicide and Life-Threatening Behavior, 44,* 569–581.

Nielsen, M., & Slaughter, V. (2007). Multiple motivations for imitation in infancy. In C. L. Nehaniv & K. Dautenhahn (Eds.), *Imitation and social learning in robots, humans and animals* (pp. 343–359). New York, NY: Cambridge University Press.

Niezen, R. (2009). Suicide as a way of belonging: Causes and consequences of cluster suicides in Aboriginal communities. In L. J. Kirmayer & G. G. Valaskakis (Eds.), *Healing traditions: The mental health of Aboriginal peoples in Canada* (pp. 178–195). Vancouver, BC: University of British Columbia press.

Niezen, R. (2014). Gabriel Tarde's publics. *History of the Human Sciences, 27,* 41–59.

Niezen, R. (in press). The Durkheim-Tarde debate and the social study of Aboriginal youth suicide. *Transcultural Psychiatry, 52*(1), 96–114.

Nisbett, R. E. (2003). *The geography of thought: How Asians and Westerners think differently . . . and why.* New York, NY: The Free Press.

Nishida, H. (2005). Cultural schema theory. In W. B. Gudykunst (Ed.), *Theorizing about intercultural communication* (pp. 401–418). Thousand Oaks, CA: Sage.

Nock, M. K., Borges, G., Bromet, E. J., Alonso, J., Angermeyer, M., Beautrais, A., . . . & Williams, D. (2008). Cross-national prevalence and risk factors for suicidal ideation, plans, and attempts. *The British Journal of Psychiatry, 192,* 98–105.

Nourse, J. E. (1879).*Narrative of the second Arctic expedition made by Charles F. Hall: His voyage to Repulse Bay, sledge journeys to the straits of Fury and Hecla and to King William's Land, and residence among the Eskimos.*

O'Dea, J. J. (1882). *Suicide: Studies on its philosophy, causes, and prevention.* New York, NY: G. P. Putnam's Sons.

Olkinuora, M. (1984). Psychogenic epidemics and work. *Scandinavian Journal of Work, Environment, and Health, 10,* 501–504.

Osafo, J., Akotia, C. S., Hjeleland, H., & Knizek, B. L. (2017). From condemnation to understanding: Views on suicidal behavior in Ghana in transition. *Death Studies, 41*(8), 532–541.

Oughourlian, J.-M. (2016). *The mimetic brain.* East Lansing, MI: Michigan State University Press.

Oyserman, D., & Lee, S. W.-S. (2007). Priming "culture": Culture as situated cognition. In S. Kitayama & D. Cohen (Eds.), *Handbook of cultural psychology.* New York, NY: Guilford.

Palaver, W. (2013). *René Girard's mimetic theory.* East Lansing, MI: Michigan State University Press.

Paperno, I. (1997). *Suicide as a cultural institution in Dostoevsky's Russia.* Ithaca, NY: Cornell University Press.

Paris, J. (2013). *Fads and fallacies in psychiatry.* London, UK: Royal College of Psychiatrists.

Parkinson, B. (2011). Interpersonal emotion transfer: Contagion and social appraisal. *Social and Personality Psychology Compass, 5,* 428–439.

Parsons, T. (1960). Durkheim's contribution to the theory of integration of social systems. In K. H. Wolff (Ed.), *Essays on sociology and philosophy by Emile Durkheim et al with appraisals of his life and thought* (pp. 118–153). New York, NY: Harper.

Patterson, A. A., & Holden, R. R. (2012). Psychache and suicidal ideation among men who are homeless: A test of Shneidman's model. *Suicide and Life-Threatening Behavior, 42,* 147–156.

Paumgarten, N. (2017). Singer of secrets. *The New Yorker, 93,* 1–13.

Pearce, T. (2017, July 21). What was Chris Cornell's cause of death, when did the Soundgarden star commit suicide and what was his James Bond theme song? *The Sun.*

Peck, D. L. (1983). The last moments of life. *Deviant Behavior, 4,* 313–332.

Perez, L. (2005). *To die in Cuba: Suicide and society.* Chapel Hill, NC: University of North Carolina Press.

Pescosolido, B. (1990). The social context of religious integration and suicide: Pursuing the network explanation. *Sociological Quarterly, 31,* 337–357.

Phillips, D. P. (1974). The influence of suggestion on suicide: Substantive and theoretical implications of the Werther effect. *American Sociological Review, 39,* 340–354.

Phillips, D. P., & Carstensen, L. L. (1986). Clustering of teenage suicides after television news stories about suicide. *New England Journal of Medicine, 315,* 685–689.

Phillips, M. R., Li, X., & Zhang, Y. (2002). Suicide rates in China, 1995–99. *The Lancet, 359,* 835–840.

Phillips, M. R., Yang, G., Zhang, Y., Wang, L., Ji, H., & Zhou, M. (2002). Risk factors for suicide in China: A natural case-control psychological autopsy study. *The Lancet, 360,* 1728–1736.

Phoon, W. H. (1982). Outbreaks of mass hysteria at workplaces in Singapore: Some patterns and modes of presentation. In M. J. Colligan, J. W. Pennebaker, & L. R. Murphy (Eds.), *Mass psychogenic illness: A social psychological analysis* (pp. 21–52). Hillsdale, NJ: Lawrence Erlbaum.

Pierson, W. (1988). *Black Yankees: The development of an Afro-American subculture in 18th century New England.* Amherst, MA: University of Massachusetts Press.

Pinker, S. (2002). *The blank slate: The modern denial of human nature.* New York, NY: Viking.

Pinker, S. (2012). *The better angels of our nature: Why violence has declined.* New York: Penguin.

Pirkis, J., Blood, R. W., Beautrais, A., Burgess, P., & Skehan, J. (2006). Media guidelines of the reporting of suicide. *Journal of Crisis Intervention and Suicide Prevention, 27,* 82–87.

Pirkis, J., Spittal, M. J., Cox, G., Robinson, J., Cheung, Y. T. D., & Studdert, D. (2013). The effectiveness of structural interventions at suicide hotspots: A meta-analysis. *International Journal of Epidemiology, 42,* 541–548.

Polanco, M., Mancias, S., & LeFeber, T. (2017). Reflections on moral care when conducting qualitative research about suicide in the United States military, *Death Studies, 41*, 521–531.

Pompili, M. (2018). Reflections of a committed suicidologist. In M. Pompili (Ed.), *Phenomenology of suicide* (pp. 13–30). New York, NY: Springer.

Porter, R. (1996a). Medical science. In R. Porter (Ed.), *Cambridge illustrated history of medicine* (pp. 154–201). Cambridge, UK: Cambridge University Press.

Porter, R. (1996b). Mental illness. In R. Porter (Ed.), *Cambridge illustrated history of medicine* (pp. 278–303). Cambridge, UK: Cambridge University Press.

Qin, P., Agerbo, E., & Mortensen, P. B. (2003). Suicide risk in relation to socioeconomic, demographic, psychiatric, and familial factors: A national register-based study of all suicide in Denmark, 1981–1997. *American Journal of Psychiatry, 160*, 765–772.

Quinn, N. (2011). The history of the cultural models school reconsidered: A paradigm shift on cognitive anthropology. In D. B. Kronenfeld, G. Bennardo, V. C. de Munch, & M. D. Fischer (Eds.), *A companion to cognitive anthropology* (pp. 30–60). West Sussex, UK: Wiley-Blackwell.

Rasmussen, K. (1929). *The intellectual culture of the Iglulik Eskimos: Report of the Fifth Thule Expedition* (Vol. 7, No. 1, pp. 1921–1924). Copenhagen: Gyldendalske Boghandel, Nordisk Forlag.

Raustiala, K., & Sprigman, C. (2010, August 12). Why imitation is the sincerest form of fashion. *The New York Times*, pp. 237–260.

Reardon, D. C. (2002). Suicide rates in China. *The Lancet, 359*, 2274.

Reinecke, M. A. (2006). Problem solving: A conceptual approach to suicidality and psychotherapy. In T. E. Ellis (Ed.), *Cognition and suicide: Theory, research, and therapy*. Washington, DC: American Psychological Association.

Renberg, E. S., & Jacobsson, L. (2003). Development of a questionnaire on attitudes toward suicide (ATTS) and its application in a Swedish population. *Suicide and Life-Threatening Behavior, 33*, 52–64.

Renfrew, C. (1987). *Archaeology and language: The puzzle of Indo-European origins*. Cambridge, UK: Cambridge University Press.

Resnick, L. B., J. M. Levine, & S. D. Teasley (Eds.). (1991). *Perspectives on socially shared cognition*. Washington, DC: American Psychological Association.

Rew, L., Thomas, N., Horner, S. D., Resnick, M. D., & Beuhring, T. (2001). Correlates of recent suicide attempts in a triethnic group of adolescents. *Journal of Nursing Scholarship, 33*, 361–367.

Richardson, F. C., & Fowers, B. J. (2010). Hermeneutics and sociocultural perspectives in psychology. In S. R. Kirschener & J. Martin (Eds.), *The sociocultural turn in psychology: The contextual emergence of mind and self* (pp. 113–136). New York, NY: Columbia University Press.

Richman, J. (1991). Suicide and the elderly. In A. A. Leenaars (Ed.), *Life span perspectives on suicide* (pp. 153–170). Boston, MA: Springer.

Rizzolatti, G. (2005). The mirror neuron system and imitation. In S. Hurley & N. Chater (Eds.), *Perspectives on imitation: From neuroscience to social science. Volume 1: Mechanisms of imitation and imitation in animals* (pp. 55–76). Cambridge, MA: MIT Press.

Roach, E. S., & Langley, R. L. (2004). Episodic neurological dysfunction due to mass hysteria. *Archives of Neurology, 61*, 1269–1272.

Robbins, T. (1989). The historical antecedents of Jonestown: The sociology of martyrdom. In R. Moore & F. McGehee (Eds.), *New religious movements, mass suicide, and people's temple: Scholarly perspectives on a tragedy* (pp. 51–76). Lewiston, NY: Edwin Mellen Press.

Rodriguez Andres, A., & Hempstead, K. (2011). Gun control and suicide: The impact of state firearm regulations in the United States, 1995–2004. *Health Policy, 101*, 95–103.

Roediger, H. L., Meade, M. L., & Bergman, E. T. (2001). Social contagion of memory. *Psychonomic Bulletin and Review, 8*, 365–371.

Romer, D., Jamieson, P. E., & Jamieson, K. H. (2006). Are new reports of suicide contagious? A stringent test in six U.S. cities. *Journal of Communication, 56*, 253–270.

Rorty, A. O. (1995). Understanding others. In L. Rosen (Ed.), *Other intentions: Cultural contexts and the attribution of inner states* (pp. 203–223). Santa Fe, NM: School of American Research Press.

Rosaldo, M. Z. (1984). Toward an anthropology of self and feeling. In R. A. Shweder & R. A. Levine (Eds.), *Culture theory: Essays on mind, self, and emotion* (pp. 37–157). Cambridge, UK: Cambridge University Press.

Rosaldo, R. I. (1999). A note on Geertz as a cultural essayist. In S. B. Ortner (Ed.), *The fate of "culture": Geertz and beyond* (pp. 30–34). Berkeley, CA: University of California Press.

Rosen, B. K. (1981). Suicide pacts: A review. *Psychological Medicine, 11*, 525–533.

Rosen, L. (Ed.). (1995). *Other intentions: Cultural contexts and the attribution of inner states*. Santa Fe, NM: School of American Research Press.

Rosenberg, C. E. (1992). *Explaining epidemics and other studies in the history of medicine*. New York, NY: Cambridge University Press.

Ross, N. (2004). *Culture and cognition: Implications for theory and method*. Thousand Oaks, CA: Sage.

Rowe, A. (2016). No regrets. In J. White, I. Marsh, M. J. Kral, & J. Morris (Eds.), *Critical suicidology: Transforming suicide research and prevention for the 21st century* (pp. 154–165). Vancouver, BC: University of British Columbia Press.

Roy, A., Rylander, G., & Sarchiapone, M. (1977). Genetics of suicide: Family studies and molecular genetics. *Annals of the New York Academy of Sciences, 836*, 135–157.

Roy, D., Hazarika, S., Bhattacharya, A., Nath, K., & Saddichha, S. (2011). Koro: Culture bound or mass hysteria? *Australian and New Zealand Journal of Psychiatry, 45*, 683.

Rubenstein, D. H. (1983). Epidemic suicide among Micronesian adolescents. *Social Science and Medicine, 17*, 657–665.

Rudé, G. (1995 [1981]). *The crowd in history: A study of popular disturbances in France and England* (rev. ed., pp. 1730–1848). London, UK: Serif.

Russell, S. T., & Joyner, K. (2001). Adolescent sexual orientation and suicide risk: Evidence from a national study. *American Journal of Public Health, 91*, 1276–1281.

Salisbury, J. E. (1997). *Perpetua's passion: The death and memory of a young Roman woman*. London, UK: Routledge.

SAMHSA. (2017). *Suicide clusters within American Indian and Alaska Native communities: A review of the literature and recommendations*. Washington,

DC: Substance Abuse and Mental Health Services, U.S. Department of Health and Human Services.

Sann, P. (1967). *Fads, follies and delusions of the American people*. New York, NY: Crown Publishers.

Sapir, E. (1934). The emergence of the concept of personality in a study of culture. *Journal of Social Psychology*, 5, 408–415.

Sarno, J. E. (2006). *The divided mind: The epidemic of mindbody disorders*. New York, NY: Regan Books/HarperCollins.

Sather, M., & Newman, D. (2016). "Being more than just your final act": Elevating the multiple storylines of suicide with narrative practices. In J. White, I. Marsh, M. J. Kral, & J. Morris (Eds.), *Critical suicidology: Transforming suicide research and prevention for the 21st century* (pp. 115–132). Vancouver, BC: University of British Columbia Press.

Schafer, R. (1968). *Aspects of internalization*. New York, NY: International Universities Press.

Schank, R. C., & Abelson, R. P. (1977). *Scripts, plans, goals and understanding: An inquiry into human knowledge structures*. New York, NY: Wiley.

Schieffelin, E. L. (1985). The cultural analysis of depressive affect: An example from New Guinea. In A. Kleinman & B. Good (Eds.), *Culture and depression: Studies in the anthropology and cross-cultural psychiatry of affect and disorder* (pp. 101–133). Berkeley, CA: University of California Press.

Schönpflug, U. (2009a). *Cultural transmission: Psychological, developmental, social, and methodological aspects*. Cambridge, UK: Cambridge University Press.

Schönpflug, U. (2009b). Epilogue: Toward a model of cultural transmission. In U. Schönpflug (Ed.), *Cultural transmission: Psychological, developmental, social, and methodological aspects* (pp. 460–477). Cambridge, UK: Cambridge University Press.

Schotte, D. E., & Clum, G. A. (1987). Problem-solving skills in suicidal psychiatric patients. *Journal of Consulting and Clinical Psychology*, 55, 49–54.

Schumaker, J. F. (Ed.). (1991). *Human suggestibility: Advances in theory, research, and application*. New York, NY: Routledge.

Schwartz, H. (1996). *The culture of the copy: Striking likenesses, unreasonable facsimiles*. New York, NY: Zone.

Scull, A. (2009). *Hysteria: The disturbing history*. New York, NY: Oxford University Press.

Segal, N. L. (1999). *Entwined lives: Twins and what they tell us about human behavior*. New York, NY: Dutton.

Seligman, M. E. P. (2000). Positive psychology. In J. E. Gillham (Ed.), *The science of optimism and hope: Research essays in honor of Martin E.P. Seligman* (pp. 415–429). Philadelphia, PA: Templeton Foundation Press.

Servitje, L., & Nixon, K. (2016). The making of a modern endemic: Am introduction. In K. Nixon & L. Servitje (Eds.), *Endemic: Essays in contagion theory* (pp. 1–17). London, UK: Palgrave MacMillan.

Shneidman, E. (1969). Prologue: Fifty-eight years. In E. Shneidman (Ed.), *On the nature of suicide* (pp. 1–30). San Francisco, CA: Jossey-Bass.

Shneidman, E. (1971). Perturbation and lethality as precursors of suicide in a gifted group. *Suicide and Life-Threatening Behavior*, 1, 23–45.

Shneidman, E. (1985). *Definition of suicide*. New York, NY: Wiley.

Shneidman, E. (1987). A psychological approach to suicide. In G. R. Vanden-Bos & B. K. Bryant (Eds.) *Cataclysms, crises, and catastrophes: Psychology in action. Master lecture series* (pp. 147–183), Washington, DC: American Psychological Association.

Shneidman, E. (1993). Suicide as psychache. *Journal of Nervous and Mental Disease, 181*, 147–149.

Shneidman, E. (1995). *Suicide as psychache: A clinical approach to self-destructive behavior.* New York, NY: Jason Aronson.

Shneidman, E. (1998). Further reflections on suicide and psychache. *Suicide and Life-Threatening Behavior, 28*, 245–250.

Shneidman, E. (2008). *A commonsense book of death: Reflections at ninety of a lifelong thanatologist.* Lanham, MD: Rowman & Littlefield.

Shneidman, E., Farberow, N. L., & R. Litman, R. E. (Eds.). (1970). *The psychology of suicide.* New York, NY: Science House.

Shneidman, E., & Norman, L. F. (1970). The logic of suicide. In E. S. Shneidman, N. L. Farberow, & R. E. Litman (Eds.), *The psychology of suicide* (pp. 63–71). New York, NY: Science House.

Shore, B. (1996). *Culture in mind: Cognition, culture, and the problem of meaning.* Oxford, UK: Oxford University Press.

Shorter, E. (1992). *From paralysis to fatigue: A history of psychosomatic illness in the modern era.* New York, NY: The Free Press.

Shorter, E. (1997). *A history of psychiatry: From the era of the asylum to the age of Prozac.* New York, NY: Wiley.

Showalter, E. (1997). *Hystories: Hysterical epidemics and modern media.* New York, NY: Columbia University Press.

Shweder, R. A. (2003). *Why do men barbecue? Recipes for cultural psychology.* Cambridge, MA: Harvard University Press.

Shweder, R. A., & LeVine, R. A. (Eds.). (1984). *Culture theory: Essays on mind, self, and emotion.* Cambridge, UK: Cambridge University Press.

Shweder, R. A., Mahapatra, M., & Miller, J. G. (1990). Culture and moral development. In J. W. Stigler, R. A. Shweder, & G. Herdt (Eds.), *Cultural psychology: Essays on comparative human development* (pp. 130–204). New York, NY: Cambridge University Press.

Siegel, M., Ross, C. S., & King, C. (2013). The relationship between gun ownership and firearm homicide rates in the United States, 1981–2010. *American Journal of Public Health, 103*, 2098–2105.

Sinclair, C. M. (1998). Suicide in First Nations people. In A. A. Leenaars, I. Sakinovsky, S. Wenckstern, R. Dyck, M. J. Kral, & R. Bland (Eds.), *Suicide in Canada* (pp. 165–178). Toronto, ON: University of Toronto Press.

Sirois, F. (1982). Perspectives on epidemic hysteria. In M. J. Colligan, J. W. Pennebaker, & L. R. Murphy (Eds.), *Mass psychogenic illness: A social psychological analysis* (pp. 217–236). Hillsdale, NJ: Lawrence Erlbaum.

Sloan, J. H., Rivara, F. P., Reay, D. T., Ferris, A. J., Path, M. R. C., & Kellerman, A. L. (1990). Firearm regulations and rates of suicide: A comparison or two metropolitan areas. *The New England Journal of Medicine, 322*, 369–373.

Small, G. W., Propper, M. W., Randolph, E. T., & Eth, S. (1991). Mass hysteria among student performers: Social relationship as a symptom predictor. *American Journal of Psychiatry, 148*, 1200–1205.

Smelser, N. J. (2011). *Theory of collective behavior.* New Orleans, LA: Quid Pro Books.

Smith, G. E. (1933). *The diffusion of culture.* Port Washington, NY: Kennikat Press.

Smith, L. B. (1997). *Fools, martyrs, traitors: The story of martyrdom in the Western world.* New York, NY: Knopf.

Sonneck, G., Etzersdorfer, E., & Nagel-Kuess, S. (1994). Imitative suicide on the Viennese subway. *Social Science and Medicine, 38,* 453–457.

Sperber, D. (1996a). *Explaining culture: A naturalistic approach.* Cambridge, MA: Blackwell.

Sperber, D. (1996b). *La contagion des idées: Théorie naturaliste de la culture.* Paris: Editions Odile Jacob.

Sperber, D. (2000). An objection to the mimetic approach to culture. In R. Aunger (Ed.), *Darwinizing culture: The status of memetics as a science* (pp. 63–173). Oxford, UK: Oxford University Press.

Spinden, H. J. (1927). The prosaic *versus* the romantic school in anthropology. In G. E. Smith, B. Malinowski, H. J. Spinden, & Goldenwesier (Eds.), *Culture: The diffusion controversy* (pp. 47–98). New York, NY: Norton.

Spiro, M. E. (1984). Some reflections on cultural determinism and relativism with special reference to emotion and reason. In R. A. Shweder & R. A. LeVine (Eds.), *Culture theory: Essays on mind, self, and emotion* (pp. 323–346). New York, NY: Cambridge University Press.

Spiro, M. E. (1987). Some reflections on cultural determinism and relativism with special reference to emotion and reason. In B. Kilborne & L. L. Langness (Eds.), *Culture and human nature: Theoretical papers of Melford E. Spiro* (pp. 32–58). Chicago, IL: University of Chicago Press. Originally published in 1984.

Spiro, M. E. (1997). *Gender ideology and psychological reality.* Princeton, NJ: Princeton University Press.

Stack, S. (1983). The effect of the Jonestown suicides on American suicide rates. *The Journal of Social Psychology, 119,* 145–146.

Stack, S. (1987). Celebrities and suicide: A taxonomy and analysis, 1948–1983. *American Sociological Review, 52,* 401–412.

Stack, S. (1994). Reformulating Durkheim one hundred years later. In D. Lester (Ed.), *Emile Durkheim: Le Suicide 100 years later* (pp. 237–249). Philadelphia, PA: The Charles Press.

Stack, S. (1997). Homicide followed by suicide: An analysis of Chicago data. *Criminology, 35,* 435–453.

Stack, S. (2000a). Suicide: A 15-year review of the sociological literature part 1: Cultural and economic factors. *Suicide and Life-Threatening Behavior, 30,* 145–162.

Stack, S. (2000b). Suicide: A 15-year review of the sociological literature part 2: Modernization and social integration perspectives, *Suicide and Life-Threatening Behavior, 30,* 163–176.

Stack, S. (2000c). Media impacts on suicide: A quantitative review of 293 findings. *Social Science Quarterly, 81,* 957–971.

Stack, S. (2002). Media coverage as a risk factor in suicide. *Injury Prevention, 8,* 30–32.

Stack, S. (2003). Media coverage as a risk factor in suicide. *Journal of Epidemiology and Community Health, 57,* 238–240.

Stack, S. (2015). Methods of suicide around the world. In D. Lester & S. Stack (Eds.), *Suicide as a dramatic performance* (pp. 243–255). Piscataway, NJ: Transaction.

Stack, S., & Bowman, B. (2012). *Suicide movies: Social patterns 1900–2009.* Cambridge, MA: Hogrefe.

Stack, S., Bowman, B., & Niederkrotenhaler, T. (2018, April)). *Explaining suicide in a leading suicide hot spot: AOKIGHARA (Japan's Black Forest).* Annual conference of the American Association of Suicidology, Washington, DC.

Stack, S., & Kposowa, A. J. (2008). The association of suicide rates with individual-level suicide attitudes: A cross-national analysis. *Social Science Quarterly, 89,* 39–59.

Stahl, S. M. (1982). Illness as an emergent norm or doing what comes naturally. In M. J. Colligan, J. W. Pennebaker, & L. R. Murphy (Eds.), *Mass psychogenic illness: A social psychological analysis* (pp. 183–198). Hillsdale, NJ: Lawrence Erlbaum.

Staples, J. (2012). Suicide in South Asia: Ethnographic perspectives. *Contributions to Indian Sociology, 46,* 1–28.

Staples, J., & Widger, T. (Eds.). (2012a). Ethnographies of suicide. *Culture, Medicine, and Psychiatry, 36*(2).

Staples, J., & Widger, T. (2012b). Situating suicide as an anthropological problem: Ethnographic approaches to understanding self-harm and self-inflicted death. *Culture, Medicine and Psychiatry, 36,* 183–203.

Stein, D., Witzum, E., Brom, D., DeNour, A. K., & Elizur, A. (1992). The association between adolescents' attitudes toward suicide and their psychosocial background and suicidal tendencies. *Adolescence, 27,* 949–959.

Steinmetz, S. R. (1894). Suicide among primitive peoples. *American Anthropologist, A7,* 137–145.

Stets, J. E., & Burke, P. J. (2003). A sociological approach to self and identity. In M. R. Leary & J. P. Tangney (Eds.), *Handbook of self and identity* (pp. 128–152). New York, NY: Guilford.

Stigler, J. W., Shweder, R. A., & Herdt, G. (Eds.). (1990). *Cultural psychology: Essays on comparative human development.* New York, NY: Cambridge University Press.

Stocking, G. W. (1992a). *The ethnographer's magic and other essays in the history of anthropology.* Madison, WI: University of Wisconsin Press.

Stocking, G. W. (1992b). Polarity and plurality: Franz Boas as psychological anthropologist. In T. Schwartz, G. M. White, & C. A. Lutz (Eds.), *New directions in psychological anthropology* (pp. 311–323). Cambridge, UK: Cambridge University Press.

Strang, D., & Soule, S. A. (1998). Diffusion in organizations and social movements: From hybrid corn to poison pills. *Annual Review of Sociology, 24,* 265–290.

Strathern, M. (2016). Afterword: Taking relationality to extremes. In L. Broz & D. Münster (Eds.), *Suicide and agency: Anthropological perspectives on self-destruction, personhood, and power* (pp. 205–212). Burlington, VT: Ashgate.

Strauss, C. (1992). Models and motives. In R. D'Andrade & C. Struass (Eds.), *Human motives and cultural models* (pp. 1–20). New York, NY: Cambridge University Press.

Strauss, C., & Quinn, N. (1997). *A cognitive theory of cultural meaning.* New York, NY: Cambridge University Press.

Sugarman, J., & Martin, J. (2010). Agentive hermeneutics. In. S. Kirschner & J. Martin (Eds.), *The sociocultural turn in psychology: The contextual emergence of mind and self* (pp. 159–179). New York, NY: Columbia University Press.

Swanson, S. A., & Colman, I. (2013). Association between exposure to suicide and suicidality outcomes in youth. *Canadian Medical Association Journal, 185,* 870–877.

Sykes, K. (2010). The value of a beautiful memory: Imitation as borrowing in serious play at making mortuary sculptures in New Ireland. In M. Candea (Ed.), *The social after Gabriel Tarde: Debates and assessments* (pp. 62–79). New York, NY: Routledge.

Szasz, T. (1999). *Fatal freedom: The ethics and politics of suicide.* Westport, CT: Praeger.

Takahashi, Y. (1988). Aokigahara-Jukai: Suicide and amnesia in Mt. Fuji's black forest. *Suicide and Life-Threatening Behavior, 18,* 164–175.

Takahashi, Y. (1989). Mass suicide by members of the Japanese Friend of the Truth Church. *Suicide and Life-Threatening Behavior, 19,* 289–296.

Takahashi, Y. (1997). Culture and suicide: From a Japanese psychiatrist's perspective. *Suicide and Life-Threatening Behavior, 27,* 137–146.

Tarde, G. (1903). *The laws of imitation* (E. C. Parsons, Trans.). New York, NY: Henry Holt and Company.

Tarde, G. (1904). *La logique sociale* (3rd ed.). Paris: Félix Alcan.

Tarde, G. (1969). Extra-logical laws of imitation. In T. N. Clark (Ed.), *Gabriel Tarde on communication and social influence* (pp. 185–188). Chicago, IL: University of Chicago Press. Originally published in 1888.

Tatz, C. (2017). *Australia's unthinkable genocide.* Canberra, AU: Xlibris.

Taussig, M. T. (1993). *Mimesis and alterity: A particular history of the senses.* New York, NY: Routledge.

Taylor, S. (1994). Suicide and social theory. In D. Lester (Ed.) *Emile Durkheim: Le Suicide One hundred years later* (pp. 1–10). Philadelphia, PA: The Charles Press.

Teo, T. (2017). From psychological science to the psychological humanities: Building a general theory of subjectivity. *Review of General Psychology, 21,* 281–291.

Thomson, O. (1999). *Easily led: A history of propaganda.* Gloucestershire, UK: Sutton.

Throop, C. J. (2003). On crafting a cultural mind: A comparative assessment of some recent theories of "internalization" in psychological anthropology. *Transcultural Psychiatry, 40,* 109–139.

Tolman, C. W. (1998). *Sumus ergo sum:* The ontology of self and how Descartes got it wrong. In W. E. Smythe (Ed.), *Toward a psychology of persons* (pp. 3–24). Mahwah, NJ: Lawrence Erlbaum Associates.

Tomasello, M. (1999). *The cultural origins of human cognition.* Cambridge, MA: Harvard University Press.

Tomasello, M., Kruger, A. C., & Ratner, H. H. (1993). Cultural learning. *Behavioral and Brain Sciences, 16,* 495–511.

Tomasi, L. (2000). Emile Durkheim's contribution to the sociological explanation of suicide. In W. S. F. Pickering & G. Walford (Eds.), *Durkheim's Suicide: A century of research and debate* (pp. 11–21). London, UK: Routledge.

Too, L. S., Pirkis, J., Milner, A., Bugeja, L., & Spittal, M. J. (2017). Railway suicide clusters: How common are they and what predicts them? *Injury Prevention, 23,* 328–338.

Toomela, A. (1996). How culture transforms mind: A process of internalization. *Culture and Psychology, 2*, 285–305.

Trigger, B. G. (1994). Ethnicity: An appropriate concept for archaeology? *Fennoscandia Archaeologica, 11*, 100–103.

Trommsdorff, G. (2009). Intergenerational relations and cultural transmission. In U. Schönpflug (Ed.), *Cultural transmission: Psychological, developmental, social, and methodological aspects* (pp. 126–160). New York, NY: Cambridge University Press.

Twenge, J. M., & Campbell, W. K. (2009). *The narcissism epidemic: Living in the age of entitlement.* New York, NY: Free Press.

Ugander, J., Backstrom, L., Marlow, C., & Kleinberg, J. (2012). Structural diversity in social contagion. *Proceedings of the National Academy of Sciences of the United States of America, 109*, 5962–5966.

Vaillant, G. E. (2003). Mental health. *American Journal of Psychiatry, 160*, 1373–1384.

Valsiner, J., & van der Veer, R. (2000). *The social mind: Construction of the idea.* New York, NY: Cambridge University Press.

Valsiner, J., & van der Veer, R. (2010). *The social mind: Construction of the idea.* New York, NY: Cambridge University Press.

van Hooff, A. J. L. (1900). *From autothanasia to suicide: Self-killing in classical antiquity.* London, UK: Routledge.

Van Orden, K. A., Cukrowicz, K. C., Braithwaite, S. R., Selby, E. A., & Joiner, T. E. (2010). The interpersonal theory of suicide. *Psychological Review, 117*, 575–600.

Van Orden, K. A., Witte, T. K., Gordon, K. H., Bender, T. W., & Joiner, T. E. (2008). Suicidal desire and the capability for suicide: Tests of the interpersonal-psychological theory of suicidal behavior among adults. *Journal of Consulting and Clinical Psychology, 76* (1), 72–83.

Voegelin, E. W. (1937). Suicide in Northeastern California. *American Anthropologist, 39*, 375–383.

Vygotsky, L. S. (1978). *Mind in society: The development of higher psychological processes* (M. Cole, V. Jogn-Steiner, S. Scribner, & E. Souberman, Eds.). Cambridge, MA: Harvard University Press.

Wakefield, J. C., & Demazeux, S. (2016). *Sadness of depression? International perspectives on the depression epidemic and its meaning.* New York, NY: Springer.

Walker, R. L., Townley, G. E., & Asiamah, D. D. (2008). Suicide prevention in U.S. ethnic minority populations. In F. T. L. Leong & M. M. Leach (Eds.), *Suicide among racial and ethnic minority groups: Theory, research, and practice* (pp. 203–227). New York, NY: Routledge.

Wallace, J. N. (1926 [1720]). *Twenty years of York Factory, 1694–1714: Jérémie's account of Hudson Strait and Bay* (R. Douglas, Trans. from French 1720). Ottawa, ON: Thorburn and Abbott.

Walters, R. H. (1968). Some conditions facilitating the occurrence of imitative behavior. In E. C. Simmel, R. A. Hoppe, & G. A. Milton (Eds.), *Social facilitation and imitative behavior* (pp. 7–30). Boston, MA: Allyn and Bacon.

Wang, Q., & Ross, M. (2007). Culture and memory. In S. Kitayama & D. Cohen (Eds.), *Handbook of cultural psychology* (pp. 645–667). New York, NY: Guilford.

Weber, M. (2011). *Methodology of social sciences* (E. A. Shils & H. A. Finch, Trans.). New York, NY: Routledge. Original published in 1949.

Wedenoja, W., & Sobo, E. J. (1997). Unconscious motivation and culture. In D. Munro, J. F. Shumaker, & S. C. Carr (Eds.), *Motivation and culture* (pp. 159–177). New York, NY: Routledge.

Wedge, M. (2015). *A disease called childhood: Why ADHD became an American epidemic.* New York, NY: Penguin.

Weishaar, M. E., & Beck, T. (1992). Clinical and cognitive predictors of suicide. In R. W. Maris, A. L. Berman, J. T. Maltsberger, & R. I. Yufit (Eds.), *Assessment and prediction of suicide* (pp. 467–483). New York, NY: Guilford.

Wenegrat, B. (2001). *Theater of disorder: Patients, doctors, and the construction of illness.* New York, NY: Oxford University Press.

Wertsch, J. V. (1985). *Vygotsky and the social formation of mind.* Cambridge, MA: Harvard University Press.

Wessely, S. (1987). Mass hysteria: Two syndromes? *Psychological Medicine, 17,* 109–120.

Wetzel, R. D., Margulies, T., Davis, R., & Karam, E. (1980). Hopelessness, depression, and suicide intent. *The Journal of Clinical Psychiatry, 41,* 159–160.

Wexler, L. M., & Gone, J. P. (2016). Exploring possibilities for Indigenous suicide prevention: Responding to cultural understandings and practices. In J. White, I. Marsh, M. J. Kral, & J. Morris (Eds.), *Critical suicidology: Transforming suicide research and prevention for the 21st century* (pp. 56–70). Vancouver, BC: University of British Columbia Press.

Weyer, E. M., Jr. (1932). *The Eskimos: Their environment and folkways.* New Haven, CT: Yale University Press.

Whitaker, R. (2010). *Anatomy of an epidemic: Magic bullets, psychiatric drugs, and the astonishing rise of mental illness in America.* New York, NY: Broadway Books.

White, J. (2016). Reimagining youth suicide prevention. In J. White, I. Marsh, M. J. Kral, & J. Morris (Eds.), *Critical suicidology: Transforming suicide research and prevention for the 21st century* (pp. 244–263). Vancouver, BC: University of British Columbia Press.

White, J. (2017). What can critical suicidology *do*? *Death Studies, 8,* 472–480.

White, J. Marsh, I. Kral, M. J., & Morris, J. (2016). *Critical suicidology: Transforming suicide research and prevention for the 21st century.* Vancouver, BC: University of British Columbia Press.

Whitehead, A. N. (1933). *Adventures of ideas.* New York, NY: Macmillan.

Widger, T. (2012). Suffering, frustration, and anger: Class, gender and history in Sri Lankan suicide stories. *Culture, Medicine and Psychiatry, 36,* 225–244.

Widger, T. (2015). Learning suicide and the limits of agency: Children's "suicide play" in Sri Lanka. In L. Broz & D. Münster (Eds.), *Suicide and agency: Anthropological perspectives on self-destruction, personhood, and power.* (pp. 165–182). Burlington, VT: Ashgate.

Wiebe, D. J. (2003). Homicide and suicide risks associated with firearms in the home: A national case-control study. *Annals of Emergency Medicine, 41,* 771–782.

Willerslev, R. (2007). *Soul hunters: Hunting, animism, and personhood among the Siberian Yukaghirs.* Berkeley, CA: University of California Press.

Wilson, J. Q., & Herrnstein, R. J. (1985). *Crime and human nature: The definitive study of the causes of crime.* New York, NY: Simon & Schuster.

Wilson, K. G., Stelzer, J., Bergman, J. N., & Kral, M. J. (1995). Problem solving, stress, and coping in adolescent suicide attempts. *Suicide and Life-Threatening Behavior, 25,* 241–252.

Winslow, F. (1972). *The anatomy of suicide.* Boston, MA: Milford House. Originally published in 1840.

Winterrowd, E., Canetto, S. S., & Benoit, K. (2015). Permissive beliefs and attitudes about older adult suicide: A suicide enabling script? *Aging and Mental Health, 19,* 1–9.

Wohlschlager, A., & Bekkering, H. (2002). Is human imitation based on a mirror-neuron system? Some behavioural evidence. *Experimental Brain Research, 143,* 335–341.

Wong, J. P. S., Stewart, S. M., Ho, S. Y., & Lam, T. H. (2005). Exposure to suicide and suicidal behaviors among Hong Kong adolescents. *Social Science and Medicine, 61,* 591–599.

Wyman, L. C., & Thorne, B. (1945). Notes on Navaho suicide. *American Anthropologist, 47,* 187–194.

Yap, P. M. (2018). Mental diseases peculiar to certain cultures: A survey of comparative psychiatry. *History of Psychiatry, 29,* 373–385. Original paper published in 1951.

Yip, S. F. Y. (2001). An epidemiological profile of suicides in Beijing, China. *Suicide and Life-Threatening Behavior, 31,* 62–70.

Zavala, N. L. (2010). The expulsion of evil and its return: An unconscious fantasy associated with a case of mass hysteria in adolescents. *International Journal of Psychoanalysis, 91,* 1157–1178.

Zerubavel, E. (1997). *Social mindscapes: An invitation to cognitive sociology.* Cambridge, MA: Harvard University Press.

Zittoun, T., & Gillespie, A. (2015). Internalization: How culture becomes mind. *Culture and Psychology, 21,* 477–491.

Index